DATE DUE

OCT 16 1988	
FEB 07 1989	
JUL 11 1989	
NOV 23 1989	
NOV 16 1990	
MAY 27 1991	
AUG 11 1992	
AUG 19 1993	
JUN 10 1997	
FEB 16 1995	
AUG 20 1997	
DEC 03 1997	

Schreiber Public Library

12354

1. Books may be kept two weeks and may be renewed once for the same period, except 7 day books and magazines.

2. A fine will be charged on each book which is not returned according to the above rule. No book will be issued to any person incurring such a fine until it has been paid.

3. All damage to books beyond reasonable wear and all losses shall be made good to the satisfaction of the Librarian.

4. Each borrower is held responsible for all books drawn on his card and for all fines accruing on the same.

RICHARD BIRCH

The Family Financial Planning Book

A step-by-step money guide for Canadian families

KEY PORTER·BOOKS

Canadian Cataloguing in Publication Data

Birch, Richard, 1945–
   Family financial planning

Includes index.
ISBN 1-55013-020-X

1. Finance, Personal – Canada.   2. Financial security.   3. Investments – Canada.   I. Title.

HG185.B57 1987   332.024   C87-093124-5

Key Porter Books Limited
70 The Esplanade
Toronto, Ontario
Canada   M5E 1R2

Design: Don Fernley
Typesetting: Computer Composition of Canada Inc.
Printing and Binding: Gagné Printing
Printed and bound in Canada

87 88 89 90   6 5 4 3 2 1

Contents

Author's Note

I want to thank Gord Riehl, tax partner with Deloitte Haskins & Sells, for his review of the book and for his encouragement and friendship over the past ten years. This book would not have been written without him. I am also indebted to Pat Bouwers, Lucy Terk and Sid Himmel, tax managers with Deloitte Haskins & Sells, Stephen Yeung, account executive with Merrill Lynch Canada, and Shantoo Patel of Royal LePage Real Estate for their expert review, comments and ideas. However, any errors or omissions in the text are solely my responsibility. I am also grateful to Peter Matthews who edited the manuscript.

And especially, I want to thank my wife Betsy Matthews, whose love and support helped turn an idea into a practical formula and now into a book.

A number of the essential ideas contained in this book are based on legislation in effect as of January 1987 and on pension reform proposals released by the federal government and several provincial governments in 1986. However, laws do change over time. You may want to confirm certain aspects of the law with a tax professional or an official at your local district taxation office.

Introduction

Why Worry?

How much money did you make last year?

If your household income was between $25,000 and $60,000, you were not alone. It is this middle-income group to which most Canadians belong. At this income level, we enjoy one of the highest standards of living in the world. In fact, few nations today have a greater percentage of people who are as comfortable or, one might think, as financially secure.

But let's consider other vital statistics. Wage hikes over the past ten years have just barely managed to keep pace with inflation. However, we are paying more in taxes now, so if you are still making the average wage, you may actually have been better off ten years ago.

The price of homes in a number of major cities has increased faster than inflation and faster than average family income over the past few years. In the near future, home ownership may be out of the reach of average Canadians.

Do you realize that about half of retired Canadians living alone have incomes below the poverty line? Two-thirds of these are women over the age of sixty-four. Many of these people are not accustomed to the business of struggling to make ends meet – they, too, were once "comfortable." How can this happen?

Ironically, it is often the high standard of living that most Canadians enjoy during their income-earning years that leads to a dangerous complacency about the future. Preoccupied by the more immediate demands of day-to-day living, few people actually take the time to assess what they will need to become financially secure over the long term. All too often, Canadians assume that company pension plans, supplemented by a few Canada Savings Bonds or funds built up in a savings account, will be adequate. And all too often, they're not.

Are the odds stacked against the average Canadian? Statistically, yes, but in practice, not necessarily. You probably have only two choices for more security: earn a large enough income throughout your career so that you always save more than you spend, or begin a program now to achieve above-average financial security. This second option is what this book is about.

Clearly, complacency should be avoided. But this doesn't mean that you should approach your financial planning in a constant state of anxiety. Unfortunately, many people think that they need to become – or hire – investment experts in order to build a comfortable future. Others believe that it requires a substantial amount of time and effort. Actually, nothing could be further from the truth.

The simple fact is you need only to follow a few simple principles in order to achieve a comfortable level of financial security. And virtually anyone can do it.

In this book, you'll learn that there are four basic financial goals common to most Canadians: (1) being prepared for emergencies, (2) owning a home, (3) saving for retirement, and (4) funding your children's education. Achieving these goals is simply a matter of following the seven-step financial security formula described in this book. Each step follows logically from the one that precedes it. So if you've already achieved steps 1 and 2, for example, you just move on to step 3 and proceed from there. The result is that you don't need to spend a great deal of time agonizing over financial decisions; the worry and stress often associated with financial planning is kept to a minimum.

Simplicity and ease of use are the watchwords of this book. Why? Because most of us would rather get on with enjoying life than spend time worrying about financial affairs. You won't find any exotic or risky investment strategies recommended here, just a handful of tried and proven investments and strategies that provide optimum return for minimum risk. And each one has been selected to provide you with the best protection against the two principal enemies of financial security – inflation and taxes.

How will following the seven-step formula affect your life-style? Probably not very much at all. You won't be told to start living like a miser; rather, you'll be shown how to rearrange the way you use your "extra" income – that is, the money that you don't spend on the necessities of life.

So don't worry. Just get started.

1
The Four Fundamental Financial Goals

If you were to take a survey of what most Canadians consider to be their main financial goals in life, chances are you'd find a striking similarity in their responses. The reason is quite simple: no matter what their circumstances, people share the same basic needs. For example, most of us discover early in our working lives that it makes sense to begin saving in order to buy a house. A little later on, those who decide to have children realize that they should begin to save for their children's post-secondary education. At about the same time, we begin to give some consideration to saving for our retirement. And most of us try to prepare for the unforeseen, usually by taking out a life insurance policy and squirreling away a little nest egg for emergencies.

Of course, not everyone will pursue all four of these goals. Perhaps you have decided to rent a home instead of buying one, or you might not plan to have children. However, on average, well over half of all Canadians will embrace all four goals at some point in their lives, regarding them not just as financial goals, but as "basics of life" – as important and almost as necessary as food and clothing. To ignore saving for retirement is irresponsible – after all, you won't work forever and retirement saving needs ongoing funding. Similarly, turning a blind eye to the possibility of your premature death or a long-term financial crisis is unrealistic and could prove to be disastrous for your loved ones. Owning a home is optional, but putting shelter over your family is not, and home ownership is almost always a better investment than renting. Finally, few parents would, in good conscience, refuse to give their children the benefit of a post-secondary education.

In most cases, funding the four objectives is achieved with what can be described as "semi-discretionary" income – that is, income that cannot be classed exclusively as either non-discretionary or discretionary. Non-discretionary income is income that you spend on the necessities of life, such as food, basic shelter, clothing, and certain work-related expenses. You have no choice but to spend a portion of your income on these items. Discretionary income is used, generally speaking, for recreation – a term that covers everything from vacations to gourmet ice cream to designer clothes. Discretionary income is also directed to the accumulation of wealth, other than wealth accumulated under the four basic financial goals.

In this country, there are about six million taxpayers who fall into the semi-discretionary income class – average Canadians who have no trouble funding life's necessities, but who have only a very limited amount, if any, of discretionary income. These are also the people who have, or could have if their priorities were rearranged, sufficient semi-discretionary income to apply to the four basic financial goals. In fact, most of these people have the means to fund the goals so as to achieve a very comfortable level of financial security throughout their working lives and during their retirement.

However, most are simply not developing and using their semi-discretionary income effectively. Of course, they could get professional advice on how to rearrange their affairs and how to invest this income, but it is unlikely that the potential extra return over the short term would offset the costs involved.

Most average Canadians recognize the importance of the four fundamental financial goals to the quality of their family's life, both now and in the future, and they are willing to devote whatever income is necessary to achieve these goals before indulging in discretionary spending. What they lack is a system to see them through today's financial labyrinth.

Most Canadians probably would rank the four financial goals in the following order of importance:

1. Home ownership
2. Saving for children's education
3. Preparing for emergencies
4. Retirement savings.

As you'll see in the following chapters, however, this ranking is based mostly on emotional considerations and not on dollars-and-cents reality of what will provide the greatest benefit to the average Canadian family over the long haul. That's not to say that you'll be jeopardizing your financial future if you follow the priorities above. It's just that you will find it easier, and more beneficial, to rearrange your priorities as follows:

1. Preparing for emergencies
2. Home ownership
3. Retirement savings
4. Saving for children's education.

Now, some parents may object to ranking their children's education last in their financial priorities. But keep your overall objective in mind – maximum financial security. In other words, if you achieve the first three goals, you will be in a much better position to meet the last.

Let's take a closer look at why each goal is so essential to your financial security.

Preparing for Emergencies

Perhaps more aptly described as "preparing for the worst," this goal addresses the most immediate potential threats to your family's financial security.

For example, how prepared are you for just "typical" financial calamities? What would happen if over the next two months:

- Your car self-destructs and you have to spend at least $10,000 on a new one?
- Your television explodes, your washer begins eating clothes and your dryer incinerates the ones not eaten, all of which cost $2,500 to replace?
- Your dentist informs you that your eldest child needs $4,000 of orthodontal work immediately – the day after your employer cancels your dental plan?
- Your favourite but impoverished seventy-three-year-old aunt moves in unannounced, but you do not have a spare bedroom?

Have you got $16,500 available to pay for the car, the appliances and the dental work? Would your bank lend you that much?

Could you afford the monthly payments on a loan of perhaps $500, which is more than one-quarter of the average take-home wage? And that only solves three of your four problems. Where are you going to get the money for an addition to your home? Can you afford to put your aunt into a senior citizen's apartment, assuming that she is willing and that there is one available anywhere at any price?

These are not even serious emergencies. They happen at one time or another to many of us. Less probable, but nevertheless possible, is the chance that you or your spouse could die suddenly. Would the family be able to survive financially?

Life insurance is not a popular subject. It appears to be too expensive, and often is. You seem to be getting very little or nothing in return for your monthly or annual premiums, and sometimes you would swear that you hear from your insurance agent more often than your best friend. Of course, most people try to think of life insurance – and their possible death – as little as possible. However, if family members are dependent on your income, you should be insured, unless of course you have sufficient assets to generate the necessary replacement income should you die. In fact, you might appreciate life insurance, and even your agent, a bit more if you think of it in terms of *income replacement* insurance.

Putting aside an emergency fund is often ranked first on the list of financial objectives. It shouldn't be. The cash in an emergency fund can be put to much better use as a down payment on a home or as retirement saving in a Registered Retirement Savings Plan (RRSP). The return on your investment will be far superior, and you'll still have assets that can be called upon – either by liquidating them to get cash, or by using them as security for an emergency loan. If you leave aside the emotional satisfaction of seeing a large figure printed in your bank passbook, you'll be much better off to treat emergency saving as simply another aspect of retirement saving.

Home Ownership

For most Canadians, buying a home will be the largest single purchase of their lives, and their best investment. Despite fluctuations from year to year, the value of real estate has historically kept pace with or outstripped inflation. Bearing in mind, too, that capital gains on your home are not taxed and that you are not paying rent to someone else each month, it becomes difficult to find a better or more satisfying investment.

Home ownership enjoys the number two priority among the four financial goals because, besides providing quality shelter that is also a quality investment, the equity you develop in your home can, if absolutely necessary, be used to fund your children's education or tide you over in the event of a financial emergency. In fact, a mortgage-free home is one of the cornerstones of your retirement planning.

Although some may find it difficult to believe when they look at the total amount borrowed, mortgages are designed to be completely paid off over a specific term, most commonly twenty-five years. Paying off your mortgage more quickly can be an excellent investment, but in some cases retirement saving through an RRSP comes first.

Retirement Saving

As mentioned earlier, it is unfortunately a fact that a large number of Canadians have retired on a less than comfortable pension. The federal government's Canada Pension Plan and Old Age Security benefits are designed to provide no more than about 40% of the average person's retirement needs. If you are earning the average wage, you must provide about one and one-half times what the government provides (60% compared to 40%) just to maintain your current standard of living in the year immediately after you retire. To maintain this standard throughout your retirement years, you may have to arrange to provide the equivalent of two or three times what the government pays in order to counteract the effects of inflation during your retirement years. Consider, too, the very real possibility that the Old Age Pension will not remain universally available for many more years.

Another factor affecting retirement needs is that the average life expectancy has been increasing dramatically every decade. If you are now in your twenties or thirties, there is a good chance that you and your spouse could be retired for almost as many years as you are in the work force. In other words, for each year you work, you have to make enough to support you during that year plus one year of retirement.

It is also a fact that fewer and fewer Canadians are qualifying for full pension benefits from their employers because we tend to change jobs relatively often. The result is that few people build up enough years of eligible service under the same pension plan to qualify for maximum retirement benefits. With the new pension reforms, this situation should begin to change over the next decade or two. However, those within five or ten years of retirement probably will benefit very little from the pension reforms.

While it may be easier to save for retirement once your children are educated and your mortgage is paid down, the sooner you start saving, the larger your retirement income will be. As well, you will be better able to protect yourself against the effects of inflation after you retire. We are all acutely aware of how insufficient retirement income, eroded by several years of double-digit inflation, has affected the quality of life for today's elderly.

As an added bonus, much of your retirement funding, such as the money contained in RRSPs or savings accumulated outside such tax-sheltered plans, has the same financial flexibility as home ownership – the savings can, if necessary, be called upon for another purpose.

Only after contributing to an RRSP and paying down some of your mortgage should you consider starting up a fund designated specifically for emergencies. It may be difficult to imagine why you and your family would suddenly need $10,000 or $15,000 or even $20,000, but such situations do crop up once in a while. Perhaps the best thing about building up an emergency fund is that the cash can also be used to fund your children's education. If the emergency nest egg is still intact when you retire, providing your retirement funding is adequate, you may want to use it for that once-in-a-lifetime vacation or to buy a recreational property or a boat.

How much should you save? That depends on the type of emergency for which you want to be prepared. But a common rule of thumb is that you should put aside enough to generate $1,000 in Canadian interest income annually, which is not taxable under your $1,000 investment income deduction (see Chapter 5), or to put aside an amount equal to one-quarter of your annual before-tax income.

Saving for Your Children's Education

Funding all or a portion of your children's post-secondary school education (college or university) ranks last of the four financial goals, simply because buying a home and saving for your retirement are better and more flexible investments. And besides, a college education is not enormously difficult to fund. We are extremely fortunate that the cost of a university education in Canada is not prohibitively high – in fact, it is one of the least expensive investments that an individual can make and provides one of the highest returns. Despite this, however, it is becoming increasingly probable that children will not be able to finance their college years entirely on the strength of summer earnings and student loans.

On average, the cost of post-secondary education has kept pace with inflation but has been rising faster than take-home wages. Thus, it takes a larger percentage of income or savings to put children through school today than it would have ten or fifteen years ago. In addition, high-paying part-time or summer jobs for students will continue to be a scarce commodity.

Reaching Your Goals One Step at a Time

Because most Canadians share the same four fundamental financial goals, it is possible to establish a common set of priorities, i.e., specific steps to take to achieve these goals. In other words, every financial action that you undertake can be structured in a hierarchy. For example, buying a home is always more important than saving for retirement. Saving for retirement through RRSPs is always more important than saving for an emergency or your children's education. In fact, as shown below, there are seven successive steps that will enable you to achieve your goals:

STEPS	GOALS
1. Set Up Your Safety Net	1. Prepare for Emergencies
2. Buy a Home	2. Home Ownership
3. Save for Retirement	3. Retirement Saving
4. Pay Off Your Mortgage	4. Your Children's Education
5. Invest for Security	
6. Invest for Gain	
7. Save for Your Children's Education	

Following these seven basic steps, you simply go from 1 to 2 to 3, and so on, each year until you have put all your semi-discretionary dollars to work. The more dollars you can make available each year, the more goals you will achieve and the sooner you will be assured of a superior level of financial security.

Thus, if you have dependants – these can include your spouse, children or parents – the first thing you should do is buy sufficient income replacement insurance (that is, life insurance). If you do not own a home, you should begin a savings program for a down payment immediately after you have taken care of your income-replacement insurance commitment. Once these two steps have been taken, you should then turn your attention to retirement saving by contributing to an RRSP (it is unlikely that you have any control over company pension plan contributions). Step 4, paying down your mortgage, should be considered only after you have maximized your RRSP contributions. Step 5 and Step 6, which focus on building up extra retirement savings for security and growth, should be undertaken only after you have paid down as much of your mortgage in the year as possible. Chances are that the final step, saving for your children's education, will not be reached by most Canadian taxpayers, although many do put family allowance payments aside in their children's names.

If you make it through to Step 7 in any particular year, you are achieving all four of the fundamental financial goals. However, even if you only make it to the end of Step 3, you are still well on your way. Home ownership and your retirement are being taken care of, and your retirement savings as well as the equity in your home can be used in an emergency or to finance your children's education. In some years, particularly those immediately following the purchase of a home and/or the birth of your first child, it may seem that you have no semi-discretionary dollars at all. Keep in mind, however, that simply by having bought a home, you are on the road to achieving all four of the fundamental financial goals.

The structure of the seven-step formula outlined in this book assumes that the reader falls somewhere in the statistical middle of the Canadian population – a married person who has (or intends to have) children and who owns (or intends to own) a home. However, if you don't fit this profile, simply ignore the steps in the formula that do not apply. Since every financial action is arranged in order of priority, you will continue to be acting effectively. So if you are not married, simply ignore the points on income splitting with a spouse. Similarly, if you do not have children and plan not to have any, just ignore the points on saving for children's education. But if you don't own a home, and never intend to buy one, save for a home anyway – all sorts of people have changed their minds. On the other hand, you may consider buying a vacation home in Canada, or perhaps a winter home in a warmer climate. There are many different ways that you can benefit from home ownership as you'll see later in Chapter 5.

The seven-step formula also takes into account the fact that priorities change during one's working life. For example, as you approach retirement, it becomes increasingly important to pay down your mortgage if you have not already done so, as well as to protect the value of assets that you have managed to accumulate over the years. Thus, in order to protect your retirement income, you would direct your investment activities towards secure, interest-bearing investments rather than equity investment funds, which are generally more risky over the short term.

As well, once you and your spouse have reached the stage where, together, you have more than $15,000 to $20,000 invested both inside and outside RRSPs, you should give some consideration to "balancing your portfolio." In other words, you shouldn't put all your eggs in one basket. For example, if you are more than nine or ten years away from retirement, you should invest your RRSPs primarily in equity investment funds. However, if the bulk of your investing has been in equity funds for the past fifteen or twenty years, it is generally advisable to begin investing new RRSP contributions in interest-bearing investments. In this way, the total value of your investments will be cushioned from the effect of a sharp downturn in the stock market.

As you'll see in the next chapter, the key to achieving real financial security is to choose only those investments that generate a secure but high rate of return over the long term. And the only way to do this is to ensure that you are staying ahead – well ahead – of inflation (increases in the cost of living). After all, if it is going to cost you twice as much to live in fifteen years as it does today, you'll want both your income and your assets to have tripled or quadrupled.

Keeping well ahead of inflation is accomplished by eliminating the tax element from investment income, and by taking full advantage of the benefits of long-term investing and the compounding of investment earnings. In fact, these very basic financial concepts underlie each step described in this book. And if you understand these concepts, you will be better able to apply the dictates of each step to your particular situation, thereby enabling you to invest more wisely and more effectively.

In summary, the financial security formula provides a framework within which you can achieve the four financial goals; it has been designed to narrow down your financial and investment options to a manageable few and present you with a system for putting these options to work in the most effective way possible over your working career. By undertaking virtually all your financial actions within the context of the formula, you will eliminate almost all decision making from the financial side of your life. Unlike other formulas or financial plans, this formula stresses implementation and simplicity, not the discussion of goals or techniques or investment philosophies. If you are an average Canadian and remain more or less average throughout your working life, the formula is structured specifically for you. It tells you exactly what to do with each semi-discretionary dollar as the income becomes available. Since you know where every dollar will be invested in advance of them being earned, you have eliminated almost all choice from your financial affairs, and therefore almost all the worry.

2
Overcoming the Obstacles: Inflation and Taxes

Planning Profile

Jim Benson is a warehouse supervisor for a large manufacturer located in Vancouver. He's in his mid-thirties, married with two children, and earns about $34,000 a year. Mary, his wife, works part-time, bringing in another $6,000 a year. They're careful with their money, rarely investing in anything riskier than Canada Savings Bonds (CSBs), and over the years they've managed to accumulate about $14,000 in these and term deposits, all in Jim's name.

Lately, Jim and Mary have been thinking that they could be doing better on their investments than the touch over 7% that they're averaging now. So they were delighted when a friend told them about a five-year Guaranteed Investment Certificate (GIC) that was being offered by a local trust company at 9%. Since the friend expected interest rates to drop shortly, Jim Benson didn't wait. He took the $2,000 that they had set aside for their next investment and put it in the GIC, in his name.

They would not have felt quite so pleased with themselves had they taken some time to calculate the after-tax return on their new investment. In fact, the yield will be only 6%. Why? Because, added to the income generated by Jim's existing interest-earning investments, the interest earned on the GIC exceeds Jim's tax-free limit of $1,000. Thus, the $180 earned on the GIC will be taxed at Jim's current rate of 33⅓%, resulting in a net return of only $120, or 6%. In other words, after making this new investment, the average yield on all their investments will actually decline.

And Jim and Mary haven't even thought about inflation, which could be 5% in the coming year. This would cut into their return even more.

The case of Jim and Mary Benson provides only one example of why every investment that you make must be evaluated in terms of how much it returns to you *after* taking into account the two biggest obstacles to your financial security – taxes and inflation. This is called *after-tax real return*. In this chapter you'll also learn about one of the most effective tools in combatting the eroding effect of inflation and taxes. It's called *compounding*, and refers to the benefits that result over the long term from reinvesting your investment earnings.

By the way, there is at least one simple solution to the Bensons' problem. Mary should invest $2,000 out of her income. She also is entitled to earn up to $1,000 of interest tax-free each year.

After-Tax Real Return

After-tax real return is a measure of the economic benefit that accrues to you over the period of time an investment is held. It is a commonly used measure and is easily the best yardstick against which to compare financial or investment options. Essentially, it allows you to put different investments on the same footing – comparing apples with apples.

After-Tax Individuals are taxed at different rates because their levels of income vary or because the province in which they live taxes its residents at a different rate from other provinces. Generally, the more money you make, the more tax you pay on each additional dollar of income earned, until you reach the highest tax bracket. Taxable income in excess of about $63,000 (in 1987) is taxed at between 50% and 60% depending on the province. Also, different types of income are taxed at different rates. For example, the rate of tax on *interest income* (earned by savings accounts, term deposits, bonds) is twice the rate on *capital gains* (profits on the stock market, for example) except that the first $500,000 of capital gains earned after 1984 is exempt from tax. Canadian *dividends* (quarterly payments made to shareholders) are taxed more lightly than interest income, and some lower-income individuals can earn Canadian dividends free of tax.

What really counts is not the investment's rate of return (for example, the interest rate paid on Canada Savings Bonds), but what is left over for you after the various levels of government take their share of income by way of taxes. Thus, if a $100 Canada Savings Bond pays $10 interest annually and your marginal tax rate is 30% (combined federal and provincial tax rate – your marginal tax rate is simply the rate at which tax is paid on the last dollar of income earned in the year), your after-tax return on the bond is $7 ($10 minus tax of $3 – 30% of $10).

Real Return If you've been in the work force for a number of years, you are all too aware of what inflation can do to your work-related earnings. So it should come as no surprise that inflation does the same thing to investment income. If inflation is running at 6% and you receive a 6% salary increase, you are no further ahead since your relative purchasing power remains the same. Similarly, to see what you really earned on your investments over the year, you should know how much of that return is offset by inflation. For example, if inflation is running at 6% and you earn 10% interest on a Canada Savings Bond, your real return (the return after allowing for inflation) is 4%.

However, this is only half the story. You also must pay tax on your earnings. So, if your marginal tax rate is 30% and you earn $10 interest on the $100 Canada Savings Bond (interest rate of 10%), you must pay tax of $3 on the interest (30% of $10). That leaves you with an after-tax return of $7, or 7%. And, since inflation is running at 6%, your real return is only 1%. In other words, on your $100 bond, your real return is only $1.

Interest on $100 Bond @ 10%	$10
Less: tax @ 30% on $10	3
Equals: after-tax return	7
Less: inflation @ 6% on $100	6
Equals: after-tax real return	$ 1

Therefore, since your after-tax real return is positive, you will be better off in the future than you are today because the spending power of the dollars you are earning will be greater. Using the above example, you had $100 at the beginning of the year, which could buy a shopping cart full of groceries costing exactly $100. At the end of the year, that shopping cart full of groceries costs $106 (original cost of $100 plus inflation over the year of 6%, or $6). But by investing in the Canada Savings Bond, you have $107 available at the end of the year ($100 plus $10 interest less tax of $3). Thus, at the end of the year, when you go to buy the same cart full of groceries, you can add, say, two pounds of apples at $.50 a pound to your grocery purchase.

Let's say your tax rate remains at 30%, but inflation edges up a point to 7%. In this case, your after-tax real return would be zero, and you could buy only the exact same cart full of groceries that was available at the beginning of the year. And if inflation climbs to 8%, your after-tax real return would actually be negative, and you would not have enough cash to purchase everything in the grocery cart. In other words, you would be worse off at the end of the year than you were at the beginning.

Maximizing your after-tax real return is at the heart of every money-making decision you make. This includes not only investment decisions, but also ones that you might make at the workplace, such as deciding whether to accept an 8% raise or change jobs. Maximizing after-tax real return is how you raise your standard of living and prepare yourself and your family for a more secure financial future.

One of the easiest ways for the average Canadian to increase his or her after-tax real return is to earn a greater proportion of income that is not taxed. Although virtually impossible with work-related earnings, it is quite easy with investment income – at least, up to a point. For example, the first $1,000 of Canadian interest and dividends you earn is tax-free, as is the first $500,000 of capital gains. And, as explained in Chapter 6, RRSPs can actually eliminate tax on your net investment.

Also, paying down the mortgage on your home is the same as earning tax-free income at the mortgage interest rate (see Chapter 7).

Returning to the previous example, if the $10 in interest earned on the Canada Savings Bond is exempt from tax, your real return will be reduced only by inflation, at 6%. Thus, your after-tax real return on the bond is $4 ($10 interest, less inflation at 6%, or $6). By earning tax-free income, you have quadrupled your real return. In terms of our hypothetical cart of groceries, you would now have $4 left over after buying the groceries, rather than just $1 – which means you can buy four times as many apples.

Table 2.1: Comparing After-Tax Real Returns

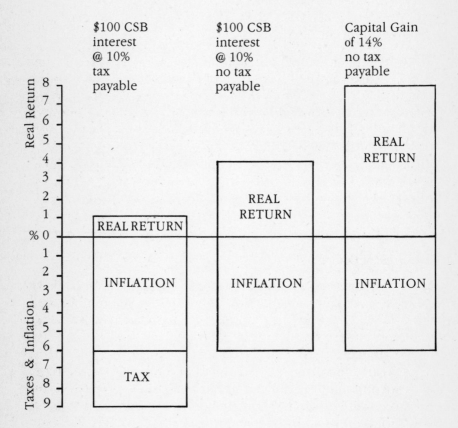

The chart above compares the after-tax real return of three different investments. The amount of real return is shown above the horizontal line, while inflation and taxes are represented in the area below the line.

- The first column represents the $100 Canada Savings Bond paying 10% interest. Inflation is 6% and the tax rate is 30%.
- The second column is the same investment, but the interest is received tax-free under the $1,000 investment income deduction.
- In the third column, a different investment is acquired which earns a capital gain of 14%. This capital gain is received tax-free under the $500,000 capital gains exemption. Inflation remains at 6%.

The investment shown in the second column quadruples the after-tax return to $4 from $1. The only way under your control to improve on this investment is to increase the earnings rate. If we assume that inflation remains constant at 6%, a factor over which we have no control, improving the rate of return could be accomplished by investing in a more risky security – say, an equity investment fund that produces capital gains. The after-tax real return then doubles to $8, although at the cost of taking on considerably more risk than with the Canada Savings Bond. Investments and risk are discussed in more detail in the next chapter and in Chapter 11.

The Magic of Compounding

Many of the investments you make will be held for a relatively long period of time. In some cases, the earnings are reinvested for you, so, in effect, interest is earned on interest. In other words, the interest *compounds*.

Not all investments compound the same way. Some compound each year, after taxes are paid on the annual earnings. Others compound before tax, since tax is paid at the end of the investment period. Some investments compound annually, while others may compound semi-annually, quarterly, monthly or even daily. The more often an investment compounds, the higher the earnings over the particular time period.

The "magic of compounding" has become a common phrase these days – and over the long term, it certainly is an apt description. For example, let's assume that you have a $1,000 investment earning interest at 10%, and you want to know how long it will take to double the value of your investment. The answer depends on how the investment is taxed and how the interest compounds. First, assume that there is no compounding (highly unrealistic unless you put the interest paid annually under your mattress, where it will not earn more interest) and tax is paid each year at 30%. It takes a little over fourteen years to accumulate $2,000 in total. However, if the after-tax return of 7% compounds annually (a much more probable case) at an after-tax rate of 7%, it takes only a few months more than ten years to accumulate $2,000. If the interest compounds monthly instead of annually, the doubling of $1,000 takes a bit less than ten years.

If tax at 30% is not imposed on the accumulated interest (which compounds at 10%) until the end of the period, it takes just over nine years to accumulate the $2,000, assuming annual compounding. This period would be shortened if the interest compounded more often. This is called *tax deferral* and is one of the primary reasons why RRSPs are such great investments.

If no tax is payable on the interest each year because it is eligible for your $1,000 investment income deduction, it would take slightly more than seven years to double your investment if the interest compounds annually at 10%. Table 2.2 shows how quickly the $1,000 investment grows to $2,000 in three situations:

- The interest is taxed each year at 30%, which means it is compounding annually at an after-tax rate of 7%.
- The interest, which compounds at 10%, is earned in an RRSP and is taxed at the end of the period at 30%.
- The interest is earned tax-free under your $1,000 investment income deduction and therefore compounds at 10%.

Table 2.2: How Long Will It Take for Your Investment to Double if It Earns 10% Compounded Annually?

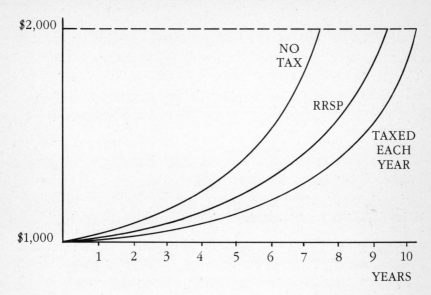

Always pay attention to how financial institutions express compounding rates. For example, an investment that compounds monthly may promise an 11% return on an annualized basis. The investment itself pays only about 10.5% compounded monthly, which produces the same income as 11% compounded annually.

These examples show the value of compounding but do not tell us what the real return is on the investment. Assume we allow the $1,000 to earn interest at 10% for ten years. Tax is payable on the interest income each year at 30%, and the rate of inflation averages 6% annually over the ten-year period. The investment grows to about $1,960 in ten years. However, these are future dollars, not today's dollars. The real value of the investment in today's dollars, after allowing for 6% inflation, is slightly under $1,100, which means that your after-tax real return is just under $100 after ten years. You should always try to think of investment returns in terms of today's dollars, the kind you know the best. Appendix C explains how to convert future year's dollars into today's dollars.

If the interest is earned tax-free for ten years, almost $2,600 would be accumulated, which is about $1,450 in today's dollars. By earning tax-free income over the ten-year period, your after-tax real return is improved by about $350.

When Is a Million Not a Million?

You may recall an advertisement that appears during the January/ February RRSP season. A young couple in their twenties decide to contribute $100 a month or $1,200 a year to an RRSP each year for forty years. Almost by magic, they accumulate $1 million in that time, and very proudly announce how easy it is to become millionaires. (Actually, they accumulate about $1,031,000 assuming an interest rate of 12% compounded annually and a $1,200 contribution made at the beginning of each year).

However, just as forty years ago a nickel would have bought you the same cup of coffee for which you just paid $.75, $1 million in the year 2027 is not the same as $1 million in 1987. In fact, if you could put $11,080 in an RRSP tomorrow and have it earn 12% compounded annually, you would accumulate about $1,031,000 in forty years. (Don't forget that tax is payable on the entire $1,031,000 as it is withdrawn from the RRSP as retirement income).

This exercise vividly demonstrates the magic of compounding, but it does not answer the crucial question – what is that $1,031,000 really worth in today's dollars? Or what is the real return on the RRSP investment after forty years? If inflation averages 12% over forty years, the same as the earnings rate, the real value of the investment is obviously $11,080, the same amount that we determined could be invested to grow to over a million.

However, if the RRSP is earning interest at 12%, it would be more reasonable to assume an average inflation rate of about 8%. In this case, the $1,031,000 accumulated in the RRSP would be worth about $47,460 expressed in today's dollars (tax is ignored since it would be paid over a number of years as the RRSP retirement income is received). This is not nearly as impressive as "being a millionaire," and in fact that "million" would buy a monthly retirement income in the form of an annuity of just under $500* (in today's dollars), which would be taxable.

Thus, if you want to retire on an RRSP income equivalent to $3,000 a month in today's dollars, and you think inflation will average 8% for forty years, you must accumulate more than $6 million in your RRSP. However, if you think inflation will average only 6%, and you can still earn 12% annually, you will have to accumulate only about $3 million in forty years to fund an RRSP monthly retirement income of about $3,000 in today's dollars. This could be accomplished by contributing approximately $3,500 annually to the RRSP over the forty-year period.

While the advertisement is factual in every respect, it does not tell the whole story, or even the most important part of the story. The question should always be asked: what is the value of the RRSP in today's dollars and what will the RRSP do for you when you want to use it? Put another way, what kind of retirement income will it buy in today's dollars? Simpler still, what is the real return on the investment?

Your Battle Against Inflation

It seems that many Canadians are becoming complacent about inflation and the effect it may have on their future. The annual inflation rate has been around 4% for several years and – for now, at least – shows no signs of soaring back up to the double-digit range we experienced in the late 1970s and early 1980s. However, experts say that inflationary pressures haven't left us. Hence, we have had relatively high interest rates that act to keep the lid on inflationary expectations. It is not clear when, or even if, inflation will hit double-digits again, but it seems reasonable to assume that wage hikes will not outpace the next bout of

---

* It is assumed here and elsewhere that $50,000 of RRSP funds at age sixty-five will buy a fully taxable life annuity with a guaranteed ten-year term paying about $500 a month or $6,000 a year, the rate in effect at the end of 1986. A joint annuity on the lives of both a husband and wife will pay less. As well, the annuity payment will be smaller if the guaranteed payout period is extended.

Table 2.3: How Easy Is It to Lose Ground Against Inflation?*

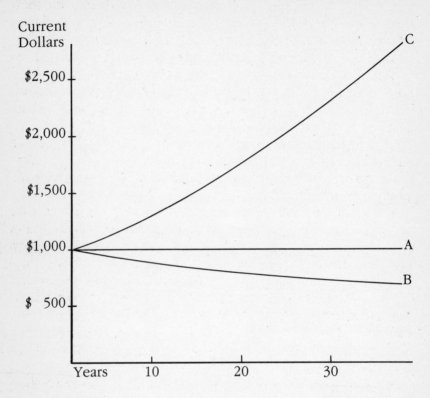

A) Savings Account – 6% – Tax-Free
B) Deposit Receipts – 8% – Taxable (35% tax rate)
C) Canada Savings Bond – 9% – Tax-Free

---

* Investment earnings are based on an average 6% annual rate of inflation.

escalating prices as they did last decade. In other words, over the next ten or twenty years it will be much easier for you to lose ground against inflation. Therefore, you should plan to get the most out of your investments now and over the long haul.

Table 2.3 examines the effect of inflation over a period of thirty years on three different investments. One thousand dollars is invested in each and income is earned annually. Inflation is assumed to average 6% annually while the tax rate is 35%. Investment A is a savings account that pays interest at the rate of 6% compounded annually. The interest is considered to be received tax-free under the $1,000 investment income deduction. Investment B is a series of deposit receipts that pay interest at an average rate of 8% compounded annually. This interest is considered to be taxable each year. Investment C is a series of Canada Savings Bonds that pay interest at an average rate of 9% compounded annually. This interest is received tax-free under the $1,000 investment income deduction.

As you can see, with Investment A you break even, because the earnings rate and the inflation rate are the same. With Investment B, you are actually worse off, even though the deposit receipts pay a higher rate of interest than the savings account. Tax reduces the net return and actually produces a negative real return over the long term. The CSBs are the best investment if the interest is not taxed. However, only $1,000 of such tax-free interest can be earned each year. If you already have $1,000 of income from other sources eligible for the $1,000 deduction, the CSB interest is taxable and your real return is negative.

Thus, to gain any ground against inflation, you need investments with a better return. In Table 2.4, two other investments are compared with the CSBs that earn tax-free interest. Investment D summarizes the results of paying down $1,000 on a 12% mortgage so that $120 of mortgage interest is eliminated each year (see Chapter 7 for a discussion of why this is such a good investment). Investment E is a $1,000 investment in an equity investment fund that produces capital gains at the rate of 15% each year compounded annually. The gain is exempt from tax under the $500,000 capital gains exemption. (Investment E could also be a net investment in an RRSP that earns 15% compounded annually. See Chapter 6 for an explanation of why RRSPs eliminate tax.)

Table 2.4: Gaining Ground Against Inflation*

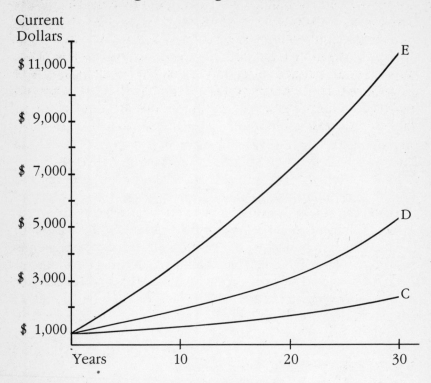

C) Canada Savings Bond – 9% – Tax-Free
D) Mortgage Paydown – 12% – Tax-Free
E) Equity Fund – 15% – Tax-Free

---

* Investment earnings are based on an average 6% annual rate of inflation.

With these two new investments, one completely risk-free, you are now making serious headway against inflation. You are more than twice as well off paying down the mortgage as buying the CSBs, and you are five times better off with the equity fund compared to the CSBs.

Put Time on Your Side The longer you can put your money to work, the more you'll benefit from the magic of compounding. If you invest about $3,400 and earn 8% after-tax compounded annually, your investment will grow to about $5,000 in five years' time. However, if you had invested fifteen years ago and earned 12% after-tax compounded annually, you could have put aside as little as $500 and still have accumulated $5,000 after a twenty-year period. The higher earnings rate helps, but the most important factor on your side is *time*.

3
Start with Common Sense

Planning Profile

Jack and Eva Howlett are like a lot of other Canadian couples. They are in their mid-thirties and have two children. Jack is a district sales manager for an industrial equipment distributor in Edmonton and earns about $32,000 a year. Eva, who works part-time at a local jewellery store, brings in an extra $13,000 annually.

The Howletts own their home, worth about $120,000 and owe $75,000 on the mortgage. In addition, they owe about $3,000 on credit cards, which carry interest at an average rate of 22% annually, and they are still financing their two-year-old car with a 14% bank loan. The $15,000 they have in an RRSP earns about 7%, their $11,000 in Canada Savings Bonds earns slightly more, at 8%, and the $8,000 or so they have spread over a number of bank accounts returns about 5% interest. Jack has had a life insurance policy for several years, which he thinks is worth "a few thousand."

If you were to ask the Howletts about their financial situation, you wouldn't hear too many complaints. Neither Jack nor Eva have much interest in finances and, as long as there's money in the bank, they're unlikely to change. Nevertheless, they do wonder sometimes why they're not a bit further ahead. And they often joke about the number of New Year's resolutions that they've made to start saving an extra $2,000 a year. Usually, they've forgotten about it by February. "Somehow," they say, "the money just goes."

Most average Canadians do find it difficult to save. Invariably, they have a smaller amount of their paycheques left at the end of the month than they expected. However, most Canadians do have or could have enough to make a difference. Let's look at Jack and Eva's situation again.

Most financial planners agree that regular, forced saving is the only way most persons will ever accumulate significant wealth. For example, if Eva invests every family allowance cheque she receives, well over $15,000 and perhaps even $25,000 or $30,000, could eventually accumulate for each child. The exact amount depends on the rate of return on the investments and the size of the family allowance payments, but by the time their children graduate from high school, this kind of saving could completely finance their children's post-secondary education.

Jack and Eva have yet to get around to saving their extra $2,000 a year. However, consider the results if they had begun to put this amount – which works out to about $40 a week – into an RRSP (Registered Retirement Savings Plan) when they were thirty years old. And let's say that the tax refund they received each year was also put into the RRSP. They could accumulate well over $1 million by the time they reach sixty-five, which certainly would contribute toward a very comfortable retirement.

But where do you get $40 a week? The obvious answer is simply, don't spend it. Instead, put it aside right out of your paycheque in a special bank account for the RRSP contribution. Another solution is to use the amount you might otherwise put into the Canada Savings Bond payroll savings plan at work for the RRSP contribution each year. If you buy $2,000 in bonds each year, you pay over $80 in interest. This means that you could have $2,080 plus your tax refund going into an RRSP instead.

There are other places to look for savings and other ways to better manage your finances. For example, you may be paying too much for the wrong kind of life insurance. Like the Howletts, you may have credit card debt or a car loan on which you are paying a high rate of interest, while you have cash in the bank earning a pittance. Your mortgage payments may be too low, or even too high. And most importantly, you may be sitting on the government's and the banking industry's best friend – lazy money, which is producing an extremely safe, but much too low rate of return.

Securing your financial future may involve realigning your spending priorities to some extent or taking a hard look at what you're paying in interest on debt, but for the most part it means making your income work harder and more effectively for you and your family. That's not to say you have to start living like paupers while you scrimp and save and horde your money; neither does it mean you have to spend hours a day keeping up to date on all the latest developments in the financial world.

Common sense is all it takes. As with dieting, taking financial planning to extreme limits is a recipe for failure. Keep it simple and proceed with moderation, and you'll succeed. In fact, all the tools you'll need – and that's not a great number – are described in this chapter.

Budgets and Budgeting

Not all of us need to keep a formal budget, but everyone should try to budget on a fairly regular basis. Very often, it's just a question of remembering what your financial goals are and making a mental note to set aside the funds necessary to meet those goals. Consider the following case.

Planning Profile

> Adam Morrow and Sandy McDonald work for the same company. Adam has never budgeted and it shows: he is chronically in debt, can never make maximum RRSP contributions although he always plans to, has never made an extra payment on his mortgage and actually refinanced for a higher amount the previous spring. On the other hand, Sandy has never had a money problem that she could recall. Although she is younger and makes considerably less than Adam, she has maximized her RRSP contributions every year since she started working, purchased a home three years ago and has already reduced the mortgage by $7,000. In addition, she has $5,000 in Canada Savings Bonds earning tax-free interest that she plans to use for an extended holiday "one of these years."
>
> Yet, Sandy never appears to skimp or deny herself. And if asked how she manages to do it, she would tell you she doesn't know. "I just save what I need," she says. "If I need

$2,000 for an RRSP at the end of February, I put aside $500 a month in November, December, January and February. I don't plan. The $500 is just there at the end of those months."

Actually, Sandy budgets non-stop, usually on a day-to-day basis – but she does it all in her head. She knows all her major expenses and her bank balances down to the penny. On the other hand, Adam doesn't even know the size of his monthly mortgage payment. "About $700," he guesses, "but it could be $800. I don't know for sure. You see it's withdrawn automatically from my account and I haven't balanced my cheque book against my monthly statement for some time. But I got overdraft privileges at the bank three years ago, so I'm covered."

While at opposite ends of the budgeting spectrum, Adam and Sandy illustrate several key points about the art of budgeting successfully.

1. Clearly Define Your Goals You must have clearly defined goals if you are to design and stick to a budget. Saving $50 each month is not a goal. Achieving a high level of financial security with the dollars saved *is* a goal. Sandy knows exactly why she is saving every penny. And it wouldn't be surprising if she knew exactly how she would eventually spend most of those pennies – she is that organized. On the other hand, Adam only has vague ideas about why contributing to his RRSP is a good investment and why he should pay off the mortgage on his house.

2. Tailor a Budget to Your Needs A budget must be tailored to the individual if it is to be workable. Adam obviously needs something written down on paper and in lots of detail. His spending is out of control and his financial habits are leading him into complete chaos. His case points out two very common problems most of us have experienced at one point or another. We tend to spend money before we have it – not just because credit is so easy to obtain, but because we are sure we will be earning more in the future and will be able to easily discharge any debt. This is usually the case and eventually our income catches up with our spending. Unfortunately for many of us, "eventually" is often twenty or thirty years, by which time it is too late to begin any effective planning for financial security.

Many of us also have ingrained spending habits that virtually control our financial lives and can destroy the good intentions of budgeting. Adam has made extravagance a habit, and until he reforms some of these spending habits, he will not be able to budget successfully. Changing his ways might not be easy, but it will probably be less difficult than Adam thinks.

Sandy's method of budgeting, on the other hand, suits her perfectly. She has energy to spare and leads a very full life. If she stopped to write out a daily log of her income and expenses, she just might put her budget in jeopardy. She would have to take time from some other activity, which she would undoubtedly resent, and, then possibly, pass this resentment on to her budgeting.

3. Sensible Financial Planning Is Necessary A budget must be accompanied by sensible financial planning. No one can plunge deeper and deeper into debt and save at the same time. First you get out of debt, then you save. Talking yourself into believing that diamonds are a great investment may make you look great at parties, but they probably will not see your children through college. Certain types of insurance may sound like good investments, especially in thirty years, but have you compared them with contributing to an RRSP? Resolving to save $50 a month is not all there is to budgeting. You also have to examine everything about how you spend money and ask if this is the most effective way to get what you want.

4. Develop and Use a Scorecard You cannot budget forever without knowing the results. Every budget should tell you how much you have put aside each month for your future financial security, and it should tell you how much your net worth has increased over the preceding year. In this sense, your budget is like a scorecard.

Two Approaches to Budgeting

There are two distinct approaches to drawing up a budget, each of which consists of four steps. Under the "Cut Down Expenses" method, you:

1. Total your net family income (i.e., total take-home pay);
2. Total your family expenses;
3. Determine what is left over; and

4. Figure out how to cut down expenses – or earn more income, if that is possible – so that some, or more, is left over.

With the second "Percentage of Income Saved" method you:

1. Decide how much must be left over, usually a percentage of net family income, and put it aside;
2. Total family income minus the leftover amount;
3. Total family expenses; and
4. Figure out how to cope with the shortfall in income, if any.

With the first method, you are essentially letting your spending habits dictate how much you set aside each month or year. It becomes too easy to say we have $500 left over, so that is what we save. It is not enough, but what can we do with our expenses at their current level? Here, your expenses have become the limiting factor in determining what is left over.

But with the second method, you have, for example, ascertained that over the next five years you must set aside $4,000 a year. Your current level of expenses is higher than your income, which now excludes the $4,000, so something has to give. It won't be the $4,000, so it must either be expenses or income.

People using the second method often say that "budgeting" is just another word for "waiting" – that is, waiting for income to catch up with how much they want to spend, not how much they have spent. And this is where the second method really pays off. If you want to refurnish the living room, you have to wait until the income is available, either to pay for the furniture in cash or to pay off the resulting debt. If you contemplate buying the furniture now when the income is not available, you must go into debt. (You have already set aside a percentage of income for saving.) Because your budget is balanced at the moment, this means that something else has to give – or "wait" – in order to pay off the debt. But because nothing else will give, your only solution is to wait to buy the furniture.

This second method also points out the necessity of setting a budget for a specific period – at least a year, but no longer than five years. Circumstances and goals change, sometimes radically if you consider a five-year period. It is foolish trying to lock yourself into a budget that demands you save $4,000 a year when you can just barely afford your mortgage payments. Similarly, it is too easy to fritter away excess cash when you are able to save $15,000 a year but your budget still says to save only $4,000.

Discussing how to increase the leftovers or cope with the shortfall is not within the scope of either this chapter or this book. There are a number of books and free publications on budgeting, all of which will point you in the right direction. Take the route that is most comfortable for you.

Personally, I prefer to do without all sorts of things for three or four straight months and then go back to my regular, un-monitored way of living for the rest of the year, rather than deprive myself of a few treasured things permanently. Saying no to the more enjoyable things in life for a few months usually means more television, but it also means more exercise, more reading, a variety of things accomplished, and a new interest or two, some of which have stayed with me for years. I know that I've always gained by keeping to a budget – never lost.

Keeping Score

The importance of keeping score cannot be stressed too strongly. Some of you might want to keep a running monthly total of how much you are saving and how much has been devoted to achiev-ing the financial objectives you have laid out for yourself. In this way you will know if your annual goal is likely to be achieved or if you should cut down your spending a bit more. If you are meet-ing your monthly savings goals, perhaps you should up the ante a bit, just to see what happens. A sample scorecard is presented in Appendix A.

Sizing Up Your Debt

Borrowing, in itself, is not bad for your financial health; it is what you do with the proceeds that tells the tale. If you borrow to finance a weekend in Las Vegas, chances are you will be much worse off financially the following Monday. However, if you take on a $70,000 mortgage in order to buy a house that appreciates at 8% or 10% a year, you will be laughing all the way into retirement.

If you are considering borrowing, there are two important factors to consider:

1. Are you able to repay the debt relatively comfortably? and
2. What is the rate of return on the investment you make with the borrowed funds?

You know best whether your income is sufficient to support a certain level of borrowing. You know your own spending habits, how much disposable income you have, and where you can scrimp a bit if necessary. Also, as we will see later in this chapter, if the interest expense on your loan is deductible for tax purposes, the loan will be easier to manage, because your tax savings will effectively reduce the amount of out-of-pocket interest that you pay.

The rate of return you expect generally determines whether you should consider borrowing. Some returns are more easy to calculate than others. It is relatively easy to calculate the rate of return if you take out a mortgage that enables you to acquire your home, or you borrow in order to make your annual RRSP contribution. However, it is impossible to calculate the same kind of specific, monetary return when you borrow to finance your children's education or to take a vacation. The deductibility of your interest expense is crucial in many situations when deciding whether or not to borrow.

With these points in mind, let's consider three types of debt.

Good Debt There are two specific instances where you should definitely consider borrowing when cash is not otherwise available. One is to take on a mortgage to enable you to purchase a house. Second, if absolutely necessary, use a mortgage to borrow against the home you own in order to finance your children's education.

Bad Debt One of the most common borrowing mistakes many taxpayers make is to borrow money for personal expenditures when they have the equivalent amount sitting in an investment to which they have relatively easy access. Bear in mind that the interest paid on personal borrowing is not deductible for tax purposes. For example, say you borrow $8,000 at 12% for the purchase of a new family car. Your interest payments are $960 annually (12% of $8,000). You also have $8,000 sitting in a Canada Savings Bond (CSB) earning 10% interest. You know that there is a 2% spread in the interest rates, but you figure you will pay off the car loan within a year or two, after which time you will still have the bond. In reality, the loan is costing you a lot more than just 2% of $8,000 annually.

First, let's say that your marginal tax rate is 40% and that the car loan will be outstanding for one year. Also assume that you must pay tax on the CSB interest, because you have already used up your $1,000 investment income deduction.

Instead of the loan costing you $160 (2% of $8,000), it is now costing you $480. Why? Because you must also pay tax of $320 on the CSB interest income. For it to be worthwhile to borrow for the car instead of cashing in the bond and using this cash for the purchase of the car, you would have to earn 20% or more on the bond to produce more than $960 of after-tax interest annually (20% of $8,000 = $1,600 less tax of $640 = $960). This is not likely to happen.

Even if you have all of your $1,000 investment income deduction available, in which case the CSB interest will not be taxable, you would have to earn over 12% on the invested funds to be better off borrowing the funds for the car. In other words, by paying off non-deductible debt, you are in effect earning tax-free income at the interest rate on the debt. Thus, by paying off the 12% car loan, you are in effect earning tax-free income at 12%, instead of at 10%, as you were earning on the CSB. This rule of thumb applies whether or not you have used up your $1,000 investment income deduction.

The principle of paying off non-deductible debt is explained in a slightly different manner in Chapter 7 where paying down your mortgage is discussed.

Ugly Debt There is no form of debt expense worse than credit card interest – that is, unless you happen to patronize loan sharks. The interest rate on many credit cards is as high as 28% and even the interest rate on VISA or Mastercard is about 18%. Of course, such interest is not deductible, unless you use, say, a cash advance on your VISA to purchase investments or buy something with your Mastercard that is used for business purposes. Even then, bank interest rates are much lower and probably just as accessible to almost everybody.

How ugly is the interest paid on credit card debt? Assume that you want to buy a small colour television. You do not have the

$400 available, so you use your department store credit card. What with one thing and another, that $400 is still on your credit card one year later. The interest rate on the credit card is 28%, so you have now paid $400 for the television – which you still owe, by the way – plus $112 interest (28% of $400). The television now has cost you $512.

But this is not the whole story. Let's say that your tax rate is 35%. If you had paid cash for the television set, you would have had to earn $615 to generate the necessary $400 in after-tax income after paying tax of $215. However, now you have to earn an extra $172 to pay the non-deductible credit card interest of $112 ($172 minus 35% of $172 = $172 minus $60 = $112). In other words, that $400 television set has now cost you $787 in pre-tax income, or almost double its value.

Of course, credit cards can be useful. They are convenient and most are not "expensive" at all as long as you faithfully pay off your balance each month. If you think that you are not likely to pay off your credit cards every month, at least put the more expensive (high interest rate) cards out of *your* misery – cut them up.

A Word about Interest Deductibility

Interest expense is deductible from income for tax purposes if the interest is incurred to earn "income" from a business or a "property." Borrowing for business purposes will not be discussed here. *Property* is a tax term for investments that produce "income." Included are: Guaranteed Investment Certificates, Canada Savings Bonds and other interest-bearing securities; stocks that pay dividends; and rental properties.

For tax purposes, "income" includes interest and dividends, but does not include capital gains. Therefore, interest is not, in theory, deductible if the capital property will produce only a capital gain and no other income. This reasoning generally does not apply to investments in shares or equity investment funds (see Chapter 11), because they always have the possibility of paying dividends at some time in the future.

Interest expense is also not deductible on the purchase of land unless you are engaged in the business of earning rental income from that land. Such interest expense is added to the capital cost of the land when you sell it and acts to reduce any capital gain or increase a capital loss.

Interest is not deductible on funds borrowed for personal expenditures such as borrowing to finance vacation expenses. Interest expense on a loan to purchase a family car is not deductible and neither is the interest expense on a mortgage that enables you to purchase your home. Car loan interest *may* be deductible if the car is used for business purposes or is used to earn employment income in certain situations. If you raise a mortgage on your home after you have owned it and you use the proceeds of the mortgage loan to earn income from a business or a property, the mortgage interest is deductible. Interest on loans used to finance RRSP, Registered Pension Plan or Deferred Profit-Sharing Plan contributions also are not deductible.

Interest remains deductible even though you do not immediately earn a profit on your investment or you incur a loss; you simply must have a reasonable expectation of making a profit. However, interest does not continue to be deductible after you sell an investment and do not repay the loan. If the interest rate on the loan exceeds the rate of return on a fixed-income investment, such as a GIC, you might be denied a deduction for the portion of the interest expense that exceeds the return on the investment.

Any interest expense incurred to earn income that is eligible for your $1,000 investment income deduction reduces the amount of income eligible for this tax-free treatment. Thus, you cannot, in effect, borrow funds to earn tax-free investment income and still get a deduction for the interest expense.

Borrowing to Invest

Many of today's wealthy people got that way by using someone else's money. The logic behind this is simple, although there is one major catch. Let's assume that your marginal tax rate is 40% and you have cash of $1,200. You can invest your $1,200 and earn, say, fully taxable income at the rate of 20% over the following twelve months for a before-tax return of $240 and an after-tax return of $144.

You can also borrow to invest and pay interest at the rate of 12%. The interest is deductible from income because the proceeds of the loan are used to earn business or investment income. Since the interest is deductible, you can afford to pay interest of $2,000 during the year, consisting of $1,200 from your cash on hand and $800 from the tax saving that results from deducting the $2,000 interest from your income (40% of $2,000). If the interest rate is 12%, you can borrow $16,667 and pay interest of $2,000 (12% of $16,667). You now invest that $16,667 at 20% and earn a before-tax return of $3,333, which produces an after-tax return of $2,000.

Your net profit on the transaction is now $800, ($2,000 minus the original cash of $1,200 used as interest expense) instead of $144, an improvement of $656. In percentage terms, you are 555% better off borrowing, which is exactly the route many have taken to vast wealth.

The principle of increasing the return on your investments by borrowing is called *leveraging* your investments. By using your money as interest, which is deductible for tax purposes, rather than investment capital, you are able to invest more and therefore earn more, if the rate of return on the investments is greater than your after-tax borrowing rate.

However, there is an important catch to the logic behind leverage that should not be overlooked – acquiring an investment that produces a return higher than the interest rate on the loan involves a degree of risk, perhaps considerable risk. In addition, that risk now relates to successfully investing someone else's money. To put yourself in the position of possibly improving your after-tax return by 555%, you have to commit yourself to repaying $16,667 to the bank. If your investment turns to dust, you will be on the hook for the entire $16,667. This is considerably more serious than just exposing yourself to the loss of your original $1,200. Even though the same investment may be bought in either situation, risk is much greater if you use leverage, because you have much more to lose.

Leveraging your investments can be extremely hazardous to your financial health if your investments do not work out. However, it might also lead to above average gains year in and year out, if you follow a conservative investment policy, and if you invest over the long term. The concept of leveraging the purchase of your family home is discussed in Chapter 5.

The Only Investments You'll Need

There are literally hundreds of different investments to choose from in today's crowded financial marketplace; however, the average Canadian need only be concerned with and understand eight specific investments. The emphasis is on straightforward, worry-free, conservative investing that requires a minimum of effort.

The eight investments summarized below vary in terms of liquidity (the ease with which you can turn the investment into cash) and the length of time each should be held. They are ranked in order of historic return, where savings accounts produce the lowest return and equity funds the highest over the long term. *Short term* generally means less than a year; *medium term*, one to five years; *long term*, over five years; and *extremely long term*, twenty to twenty-five years.

1. Savings Accounts Savings accounts should be considered only over the very short term. Banks, trust companies, credit unions and *caisses populaires* (all referred to as banks throughout this book) offer a variety of savings accounts, many offering daily interest. Some, often called investment accounts, offer higher rates of interest if a large minimum balance is maintained in the account. However, for larger amounts and terms longer than a month or two, you might do better with term deposits, Treasury Bills, Canada Savings Bonds and money market investment funds.

2. Term Deposits Term deposits (also called deposit receipts) can be obtained with maturities up to one year, but a minimum amount must be invested – often $5,000. Generally, penalties will apply if you cash them before the maturity date. Term deposits are available where you bank, but you can often get a better return on T-Bills, Canada Savings Bonds and money market investment funds.

3. Guaranteed Investment Certificates (GICs) These are medium-term investments, usually available in one- to five-year maturities, although some institutions offer longer maturities. In most cases, GICs cannot be cashed until maturity, although you might be able to sell one to a third party at a discount on its face value. Available where you bank and from insurance companies, GICs provide rates of return that are usually attractive and competitive among institutions.

4. Canada Savings Bonds (CSBs) CSBs can be short-, medium- or long-term investments since they can be cashed at any time. Interest is payable to the end of the month preceding the date you cash them – as long as you wait until the February following the initial purchase of the bonds. CSBs provide a rate of return that is competitive with other short-term interest-bearing investments. Available almost everywhere, they sometimes can be purchased through your employer on the payroll savings plan.

5. Treasury Bills (T-Bills) T-Bills are short-term investments with varying maturities up to one year, although they can be sold before maturity. In some cases, they may be available where you bank, and always from stockbrokers. You buy T-Bills at a discount and on maturity receive the full face value. The difference between the purchase price and the face value of the T-Bill is interest income. The size of the difference, or discount, is determined by current interest rates.

6. Strip Bonds Strips are the interest coupons "stripped" from government guaranteed bonds. They can be short- to extremely long-term investments. Very often, they can be sold before maturity. Like T-Bills, they are purchased at a discount and are generally available from brokers. Since you do not actually receive any interest on a strip – you simply receive the face value on maturity, which may be twenty or twenty-five years away – these securities are generally suitable only for your RRSP.

7. Income Investment Funds These are usually long- to extremely long-term investments. Units in most funds can be cashed in on relatively short notice, sometimes within a day or two. Income funds invest primarily in a variety of interest-bearing securities. You buy units of the fund itself and participate in these investments, which are managed by professionals. There are essentially three types: bond funds, money market funds which invest in short-term securities, and which can also be held over the short term, and mortgage or GIC type funds. Some funds are available where you bank; most can be purchased from brokers or directly from the fund itself.

8. Equity Investment Funds These are also long- to extremely long-term investments. Units in equity funds can be cashed in relatively quickly. These funds invest primarily in the shares of public companies. You buy units in the fund and therefore participate in the capital growth and dividend income of the fund's investments. There are essentially two types of equity funds: those that qualify for an RRSP and therefore invest primarily in shares of Canadian companies, and those that do not qualify for an RRSP and therefore can invest anywhere in the world. They are available from brokers, the fund itself or, for some funds, from banks.

These eight investments are explained in more detail throughout the text as the seven steps to financial security are discussed. As well, further detail on the investments is available in Chapter 11.

Five No-Nonsense Financial Strategies

Knowing eight secure, attractive investments does not do you much good unless you know how to use them. For instance, there is no point in buying a five-year GIC, no matter how high the interest rate might be, if you know that you will need the funds in two years to pay for your child's first year of college. But on the other hand, a couple who are five years away from retirement would find the GIC an ideal investment.

Similarly, if you intend to buy a home sometime over the next two years, there is no point in investing in an equity fund. Your investment could be worth less than you paid for it in two years, and your dream of buying your first home could be shattered. However, you should certainly consider investing in an equity fund as a retirement investment, since you will not need to use the money for many years.

To achieve any of the four financial goals described in Chapter 1, you need a strategy to put one or more of the eight investments to work for you in the most effective way possible. This means getting the best return over the period of time you hold the investment and ensuring that the investment can be sold with no penalties when you require the cash.

The eight investments will ensure a secure, attractive return on your invested cash. The five strategies will improve that return by eliminating any tax that you might otherwise pay on your investments. Only by earning the most that you possibly can on your investments will you eventually achieve a high level of financial security.

Most Canadians are already using two or three of the five strategies listed below. Some may be using them all. In any case, you will have heard of most of them, and perhaps you may have even considered using them yourself. What you may not know is how powerful they can be when used properly.

Strategy 1: *Maximizing Savings in Registered Retirement Savings Plans (RRSPs) and Company Registered Pension Plans (RPPs).* These plans offer the best way to defer the payment of tax to future years, thereby maximizing your savings for retirement. Contributions you make to company retirement plans are deductible from income for tax purposes and therefore your tax liability is reduced each year. Similarly, contributions to RRSPs are deductible from income and can produce tax refunds. In addition, RRSPs are flexible enough to be used for a variety of purposes, including saving for the down payment on a home or financing your children's post-secondary education.

RRSPs are available where you bank, as well as from stock brokers and insurance companies. You can also buy investment funds that are eligible as RRSPs. Another option is to open a self-directed RRSP which allows you to decide exactly how to invest your annual contributions.

Strategy 2: *Maximizing the Annual $1,000 Investment Income Deduction* The first $1,000 of interest and dividends received from Canadian sources each year is not taxed. This includes interest from savings accounts, deposit receipts, GICs, CSBs, T-Bills and any interest from Canadian sources earned through an investment fund.

Strategy 3: *Taking Advantage of the New $500,000 Capital Gains Exemption* Average Canadians, as well as the rich, can benefit from this new wrinkle in the tax system. For example, capital gains will be realized when you sell your units in an investment fund, and you might realize capital gains if you sell T-Bills or GICs before their maturity date.

Strategy 4: *Income Splitting with Your Spouse*   Ensuring that the lower income spouse always has a certain level of income can mean tax savings, and the overall return on family investments is consequently improved. For example, if you earn $1,500 of interest income, $500 will be subject to tax after claiming the $1,000 investment income deduction. However, your spouse could earn that $500 of interest tax-free under his or her own $1,000 deduction.

Strategy 5: *Ensuring Your Children Earn a Certain Level of Income*   Why not let your children earn investment income that you otherwise would earn and on which you would pay tax? The children pay no tax on the income because their total income for tax purposes is too low, and it will allow them to pay their own way through school. In 1987, your children, or anybody for that matter, can earn up to about $5,200 and not pay any tax if their income includes at least $1,000 of Canadian interest. If deductible tuition fees are being paid for their education, or they are entitled to the $50 a month education deduction, they can earn even more and not pay tax.

4

First Step: Setting Up Your Safety Net

There are two principal methods of ensuring that you are financially prepared for an emergency. One is to accumulate funds specifically for this purpose as savings, which you hope will be enough to take care of whatever unexpected financial needs arise. The other is to buy insurance that will meet your financial needs should a specific emergency occur. Both have a place in every person's financial planning.

The term *emergency* has a broad meaning and can include anything from orthodontal work on your children's teeth to the death of your spouse. If you have a generous dental plan at work, the first may require only $1,000 of your hard-earned cash; the latter may require as much as $400,000 just to replace lost family income. These are only two of an infinite variety of emergencies that might crop up and will cost anywhere from a few dollars to millions if you are on the short end of a liability suit.

Step 1 in the financial security formula focuses on only one kind of emergency, the type that can change your life. Unlike other types of emergency – which can be covered with funds built up by home ownership or retirement saving – this requires insurance.

Insurance

Few people think about life insurance when they enter the work force. If you are not married, it is probably not necessary unless you support other dependants. In fact, life insurance may still not be necessary when you get married and both of you are working. However, if one spouse becomes dependent on the other, you have children, or even if you buy a house, you should consider buying life insurance on at least the higher income spouse. If both spouses are working and you are dependent on your combined income, then both should carry life insurance. You also may want to start thinking about disability insurance, as well as mortgage insurance if you own a house.

At the same time, both you and your spouse should consider making out a will. The legal fees are minimal, and the legal problems avoided should one of you die are many. If you do die intestate (without a will), provincial law governs how your assets are distributed to your spouse and children, or to other next of kin if you are not married and have no children.

Income Replacement Insurance (Life Insurance)

The death of a spouse is the most serious of all possible emergencies, particularly if he or she happens to be supplying a significant part of the family income. And too often this results in tragic, long-term financial difficulties that only compound the family's personal grief. In fact, it can often be much more difficult to recover financially from the death of a spouse than to make an emotional recovery. That is why the purchase of sufficient life insurance should be your number one priority.

Life insurance is, and should be called *income replacement insurance*. If you, the higher income spouse should die, most if not all of your income must be replaced in order for your family to continue to enjoy the comforts of life that you intended to supply. This is exactly what life insurance is designed to do – pay your surviving spouse and/or children a lump sum that can then be used to generate a stream of income for as long as they require it.

The insurance-buying public has become much more discriminating and knowledgeable over the past decade or two, and the insurance industry has responded by issuing new products better suited to the public's needs. To its credit, the industry has attempted to make insurance more understandable and accessible, and it has become more competitive in many areas. That said, however, you should approach the world of life insurance with caution.

Term Life Insurance – It's All You Really Need

There are essentially two types of life insurance, although these are packaged in literally hundreds of variations. One type, called *permanent,* or *whole, life insurance,* is a form of investment. As well as providing cash on the death of the insured (this part is called the *mortality element),* a permanent policy provides an investment element that's something like a savings account. It builds up in value as your monthly or annual premiums accumulate – although much more slowly in many cases. The premiums you pay for this type of insurance remain constant as long as the insurance is in effect, and may actually stop once the value of the investment element equals the face value (mortality element) of the policy. When you are young and can least afford it, this type of policy is extremely expensive for the amount of coverage provided. It only becomes "cheap" later in life, at which time you can easily afford it but probably have the least need for insurance coverage. And in terms of their return on investment, some of these policies cannot even compare with savings accounts. This type of insurance should be avoided.

The other type of insurance is called *term insurance.* It does only one thing – on the death of the insured, it pays the face amount of the policy to the insured's beneficiary. It is the cheapest form of insurance available and it is what you should buy to replace lost income in the event of the death of you or your spouse. The younger you are, the less expensive it is, because statistically there is less chance of you dying at that age. Most term policies are written for a period of five years, after which time the premium is increased for another five-year term. Most term policies guarantee that you can continue buying the same amount of coverage until you reach a specific age – usually between sixty-five and seventy-five years old. Rates on term insurance vary considerably, so shop around. Non-smokers pay considerably less than smokers.

Saying No to Your Insurance Agent

Since term insurance is relatively inexpensive, it also pays the lowest commissions to insurance agents. So you will probably have to say no when the agent tries to sell you some form of permanent insurance. There are any number of ways to do this –

none of them easy – so you might want to consider the two arguments outlined below.

An accountant friend firmly believes in the school of thought that says you are better off buying the cheapest term insurance available. Then each year you take the cost of the term policy and subtract it from what you would have paid for the permanent insurance, and invest the difference. The accountant quite logically theorizes that if your return on your investment is equal to what the insurance company can earn, you will be better off because you will have eliminated the profit that would otherwise go to the insurance company and the insurance agent. And if the agent asks how you expect to do as well as the insurance company, tell him or her that you will consider putting your money into the insurance company's investment funds, several of which have done extremely well lately. You might even contribute this difference to an RRSP, which will increase the return on your investment. Or, you might consider using the difference in cost between the two types of policies as a portion of the down payment on your first home, which almost always will be a better investment than a permanent insurance policy, and certainly a more useful one.

If this argument does not sit too well with the agent, you might try telling him or her that you have no intention of paying for what you won't eventually need. If your financial plans go according to schedule, you will have accumulated sufficient assets a few years prior to retirement to provide all your family's conceivable income needs. At that point you intend to cancel all your life insurance because you won't need it any more.

Neither rebuttal is perfect, but neither will be the agent's arguments. Just remember that the agent would rather sell you term insurance than no insurance at all.

In fact, you can probably do much of your shopping around by telephone so that your only contact with an agent is to sign the appropriate papers and write a cheque.

How Much Income Replacement Insurance Should You Buy?

This depends on your personal situation. If you have no children, if both you and your spouse are employed full time, and if you have some savings, you may not want to bother buying any, or perhaps just a small amount – say, $50,000 – to cover current expenses. Of course, you should also have mortgage insurance (see below).

On the other hand, if you have children, if your family is entirely dependent on the income of one spouse, and if the non-working spouse will not be able to re-enter the work force at a high enough wage to support the family, you should have much larger insurance coverage.

Remember to check out all possible sources of insurance. For example, many employees are covered by a group policy at their place of work. You may have basic life insurance through an association or union or group of some type. And you might ask your parents if they still have a policy in effect on you. Often, life insurance carried through groups or memberships pays off only in specific circumstances. For example, you may have to lose your life while hunting or fishing, or flying an airplane, before your beneficiaries can collect. This type of insurance, which is exceptionally inexpensive and sometimes has a face value of $1 million, is no substitute for regular term life insurance.

Calculate Your Income Replacement Insurance Needs

The following Planning Profile should help you to make a rough assessment of your insurance needs. Remember to be relatively conservative when estimating your income needs.

There are two methods of determining your insurance needs. The first method simply looks at how much it would cost to replace the lost income by purchasing an annuity, and then adjustments are made to this cost. With the second method, you attempt to detail all anticipated income needs and major expenditures for the forseeable future and then determine how much it will cost to fund these requirements. An insurance agent can help you with the calculations if you opt to use the detailed method. The simplified method is outlined below.

Planning Profile

John and Debra Yong, whose insurance needs are summarized in the accompanying worksheet, are in their early thirties and have two children, aged two and three. Debra has temporarily left the work force. Family income after taxes is currently about $35,000. There is a $70,000 mortgage on their home, they have $30,000 in RRSPs, and $80,000 worth of company life insurance and death benefits on John. As well, John's parents have a $25,000 life insurance policy on John with Debra as beneficiary. John and Debra base their calculations on the assumption that John will die tomorrow.

John's income currently provides all the family's needs, but there isn't too much left over. Debra plans to re-enter the work force once the children are both in school. They expect that their combined incomes will cover all future needs and leave them very comfortable. John might have to buy almost $800,000 of life insurance to replace his income for thirty years and have it increase by 7% annually. This much insurance is obviously excessive, so Debra makes some adjustments.

If John were to die tomorrow, Debra still would not re-enter the work force for a few years. However, she would upgrade her education in the meantime in order to increase her income-earning potential. She is confident that once their children's post-secondary education is complete, she will be self-sufficient. Thus, she estimates that for the next five years, she and her two children would require a bit less income than is currently coming in – perhaps $30,000 a year – and then about half that amount for the next fifteen years. She thinks that if the income were indexed annually at 4% instead of 7%, it would still keep pace with inflation. Debra would purchase annuities with the life insurance proceeds to provide the necessary income.

An annuity is a simple contract under which you pay a specific lump sum now and a periodic income is guaranteed to be paid to you over a stated period of time. The amount payable is based on current interest rates, the term of the annuity and, if the annuity is for life, your life expectancy. All types of annuities are sold by life insurance companies, while trust companies sell fixed-term annuities.

John and Debra determine that John should carry about $250,000 of life insurance. If John is thirty-two years old in early 1987 and a non-smoker, $250,000 of term life insurance can be purchased for less than $25 a month.

Table 4.1 John and Debra Yong's Income Replacement Insurance Needs

Immediate Expenses		
Mortgage	$70,000	
Death (funeral, legal, etc.)	15,000	
Repayment of debt	10,000	
Other	5,000	
Total		$100,000 (A)
Cost of Replacement Income		
First 5 years – $30,000 a year, indexed at 4% annually	125,000	
Next 15 years – $18,000 a year, indexed at 4% annually	130,000	
Total		255,000 (B)
Total Cash Required (A + B)		355,000 (C)
Less Adjustments		
Company insurance and death benefits	80,000	
Insurance carried by John's parents	25,000	
Total		105,000 (D)
Life Insurance Required (C – D)		$250,000 *

---

* Tax is ignored in the calculations. Life insurance proceeds are not taxable currently and, hence, a large portion of the annuity would also not be taxable.

The insurance agent or company from whom you buy your insurance should be able to provide examples of the costs of various types of annuities so that you can determine the amount of term insurance you need. In addition, you should review your needs periodically (perhaps every two years) to ensure that your coverage is adequate. You might even discover that you are carrying too much insurance and can actually cut back.

Declining Insurance Needs

As you build up your savings, your need for income replacement insurance will gradually decrease. Unfortunately, many people seem to forget this, and they keep paying premiums for insurance they no longer need. Life insurance should be viewed as an investment designed solely to provide for your dependants by replacing income or assets that are lost in the event of your death. It should not be viewed as a lottery that you do not expect to win.

One of the primary benefits of achieving financial security is that you are able to insure yourself against disaster. By progressing through the necessary steps, you will eventually accumulate enough assets – whether they be a mortgage-free home, retirement funds, or specific investments – to make it pointless to pay for insurance coverage, which becomes more expensive as you get older. If both you and your spouse have accumulated enough to retire on comfortably, one spouse will certainly have enough to live on if the other should die. Of course, that assumes the surviving spouse inherits all the deceased's assets, and that pension coverage includes benefits payable to the surviving spouse.

Once you have bought a house and built up your RRSPs to some extent, you might want to consider maintaining your term life insurance premiums at their current level. Since the cost of term insurance increases as you get older, you will end up buying less insurance at each renewal date of the policy. Very often you will find that over, say, a five-year period, your net wealth will have increased by more than the decrease in life insurance coverage. However, you should still make periodic assessments of your income replacement needs to confirm that you do indeed have enough insurance. Much of your increase in net wealth will be directed to retirement saving, and this should be left intact until the surviving spouse reaches retirement age.

Disability Insurance

There's a good chance that you already have adequate insurance for short-term and long-term disability, although it may take some digging to find out the exact details of the coverage. First, the employees of many industries are covered under Workers' Compensation. The benefits vary depending on a wide range of factors, but generally payments will not be sufficient to replace lost income. Disability benefits may be available under the Canada or Quebec Pension Plans, although these will only replace a portion of your income. Short-term benefits are also available under the Unemployment Insurance Plan. If you are self-employed, however, it is probable that you will only be able to obtain benefits from the Canada or Quebec Pension plans. As well, benefits from employer-sponsored plans or individual plans are usually reduced by those amounts received from the three government sources mentioned above. Unemployment insurance and Canada or Quebec Pension Plan benefits are taxable, although Workers' Compensation benefits are not.

Many employers carry group disability plans which generally provide coverage in addition to that available from government sources. The plans may provide anywhere from 50% to 70% of your income, but may not start paying benefits until ninety days after your claim or even longer. Benefits may continue for life, or to age sixty-five, or perhaps for only six months or a year. Short-term plans may provide benefits immediately, but they last only a few months. Some plans cover only those work-related accidents that are not covered by Workers' Compensation. Generally, if the employer pays part or all of the premiums, the benefits will be taxable.

If your employer carries a disability plan and you are covered by Workers' Compensation, you should be adequately covered for almost all types of disability. If your employer does not have a plan, bear in mind that Workers' Compensation covers only those accidents that occur in the workplace.

If you are self-employed or are inadequately covered elsewhere, and your family is dependent on your income, you might want to consider some form of individual disability insurance. The cost will depend on your occupation, the types of disabilities covered, the amount of the coverage, how soon you wish to receive benefits after the date of the disability, and the length of time that the policy will run. Be sure to check out the terms of the contract carefully. Some policies may be cancelled or the premiums raised at the discretion of the insurance company. On the other hand, some policies may guarantee the annual premiums for an extended period and that the coverage cannot be terminated by the insurance company.

Disability insurance is relatively expensive, so buying a policy that you can afford probably means accepting smaller benefits than you might have expected. When you are shopping around, make sure that you compare prices on similar types of policies. Unfortunately, it is often difficult to find identical policies offered by different insurance companies. Also bear in mind that your employer, if you have one, may carry other types of insurance that provide some of the benefits found in disability insurance. Automobile insurance, for example, may also include benefits for persons injured in an auto accident.

Property Insurance

If you have a mortgage, its terms undoubtedly require you to carry fire insurance at least equal to the outstanding principal on the mortgage. But you should also consider increasing your fire insurance coverage to reflect the replacement value of the home itself, should it be destroyed. Replacement value contents insurance is relatively cheap and should be considered by everyone, including non-homeowners. Most homeowner policies also include liability insurance.

Mortgage Insurance

Although mortgages generally require that you carry fire insurance on the home, many do not require you to carry life insurance that pays off the outstanding principal on the mortgage in the event that either you or your spouse dies. If you do not have such mortgage insurance, you should acquire the necessary amount immediately, either from your mortgagee (usually a financial institution), or you could acquire no-frills term insurance on you and your spouse with a face value equal to the outstanding balance of the mortgage. Adding $50,000 or $75,000 to your term insurance is generally very inexpensive and should be compared to the cost of the mortgagee's insurance.

Other Types of Insurance

If you own an automobile, insurance coverage is generally mandatory. This is not the case, however, if you own a boat or certain other types of vehicles. The kinds of coverage available may vary, but at the least you should make sure that you have sufficient liability insurance to protect you if another person is injured or killed and you are held legally responsible. In recent years, damages in liability cases have been skyrocketing. In fact, minimum liability coverage is now generally considered to begin at $1 million.

Keep Your Insurance Costs to a Minimum

It is not difficult to become overinsured. Your agent may talk you into more life insurance than you need; you may have an individual disability policy when you are adequately covered by your employer; or you may even be carrying expensive collision insurance on an automobile that is worth only a few hundred dollars. Keep in mind that all money spent on insurance premiums is non-productive – that is it is neither earning income nor contributing to your net wealth. In fact, it is a drain on your future financial security and should be looked upon in that light.

Of course, some coverage – such as life, home and car insurance – is necessary. But disability insurance can, in many cases, be looked upon as optional. Only you can decide when enough is enough. If you are paying so much in annual insurance premiums that you are unable to save for a down payment on your first home, cut back on your insurance wherever possible. It is more likely that you and your family will enjoy good health and a home for many decades than it is you will need to make a significant claim on your insurance.

Emergency Fund

Traditionally, financial planners have placed too much importance on developing an emergency fund as quickly as possible, then maintaining it at a level of, say, three months' gross income. It is usually recommended that these funds be placed in relatively low-return investments that are secure and which can be accessed at a moment's notice.

Chances are excellent, however, that you will be much better off in the long run – and short run, too – if you use those emergency funds to buy a home first and then contribute as much as possible to RRSPs. You will also improve your overall financial security if you use emergency funds to pay down your mortgage. Only after these priorities are met should you consider setting up an emergency or contingency fund.

5

Second Step: Stop Paying Rent

You have probably heard it more times than you can remember, but it is just as true today as it was in your parents' and grandparents' day – owning a home is the best investment an average wage earner can make in his or her lifetime.

Over the last twenty years, the average resale price of a house in Toronto has increased at a rate of about 10% a year. Meanwhile, the Consumer Price Index, which measures inflation, has risen less than 7% a year over the same time frame. And, since capital gains on your principal residence (what Revenue Canada calls an owner-occupied home) are not taxable, this represents a "real" gain (that is, after allowing for inflation) of 3% annually, which, if realized on any other investment, would be relatively attractive.

While the increase in the resale value of houses nationally is not quite as good as in Toronto, the average annual gain still has outstripped inflation in many areas.

Why Homes Are Such Great Investments

The quality of the investment you make by owning a home is certainly one compelling reason for making home ownership the second step in the financial security formula. The real return is attractive, the security of your invested capital is exceptional, and a home is one of the few investments you can enjoy on a day-to-day basis.

One question often asked is why a home should be looked on as an investment when you have no intention of selling it and realizing any gain. An investment is simply an outlay you make with the expectation of increasing your net wealth. The longer you own a home, whether one or a series – the more that home will be worth over time and the greater will be your accumulated wealth.

Some investments also improve your cash flow, generally because they earn income. A home is no exception. As you pay down your mortgage, which serves to reduce the size of your mortgage payments, large amounts of cash are eventually freed up which can be used for investment purposes.

Most Canadians will own two or more homes during their lifetime. It is the equity that is built up in a home (the difference between the value of the home and the remaining principal in your mortgage) that allows you to move up to a bigger, more expensive home. At the same time, you are improving your investment and accumulating more wealth. In addition, you can borrow against the equity you have in a home, just as you can use more conventional investments as collateral, or security, for borrowing.

Your Home as a Leveraged Investment   Recalling our earlier example of resale homes in Toronto, it should be pointed out that the long-term, real return is actually more attractive than the 3% mentioned – and not just in Toronto. This is because home ownership is initially a leveraged investment. *Leveraging an investment* simply means that you borrow a portion of the cost so that only a relatively small amount of your own money is used to buy the asset. For example, you may purchase a house with a down payment of 25% of the purchase price, and a mortgage for the remaining 75%, which is simply a loan that is secured by the value of the house. As the owner of the house, any increase in its resale value is passed on to you – just as if you had paid the full purchase price. But because you paid only a small portion of the purchase price with your own funds, the real rate of return on those funds is much higher.

For example, let's assume that you buy a home for $100,000 and use $25,000 of your own savings as a down payment. If the house increases in value by 10%, or $10,000, in the first year, your gain is actually $10,000 based on an investment of $25,000, or 40%. Your real gain is therefore 33%, assuming an inflation rate of

7%.* Even the most astute investors rarely find investments that provide this kind of real return with such little risk.

Another compelling reason for owning your own home is the almost universal resistance to paying rent. In addition to getting nothing lasting in return – such as title to the property – most people resent lining someone else's pockets with their daily wages. Rents always go up year by year, whereas the day-to-day costs of owning a home generally decline over the years as you reduce the principal outstanding on your mortgage. Most importantly, the rent for comparable accommodation – that is, a home of the size and in the location you would consider purchasing – is probably out of reach of most people, particularly if they are trying to save to purchase their own home. Therefore, renting almost always leaves you with no choice but to live in "inferior" accommodation.

Finally, there are precious few investments on the market that you can actually live in. Even if, as an investment, your real gain on a home were zero, the enjoyment factor alone would make home ownership an attractive investment.

Does It Ever Make Sense to Rent?

The answer to this question is yes, but certainly not on economic grounds. Home ownership involves a certain responsibility and commitment of time and money, and not everyone is prepared to do this. Owning a condominium (see below) demands less time and responsibility, but perhaps not enough to suit everyone. It really comes down to the fact that, even though they can afford to own a home, some people will always prefer to rent, and nothing can talk them out of it.

Those who are forced to move on a fairly regular basis as a result of transfers by their employer might also be able to make a

---

* When determining the actual return on a leveraged investment, the return is generally reduced by the amount of interest paid on the borrowed funds. With a home, this is not necessary because you would otherwise be paying rent equal to all or at least a large portion of the mortgage interest.

case against owning a home. If you are selling a home every year or two, any gain could be eaten up by real estate fees on the sale, as well as legal fees on both the purchase and sale. In addition, you may find yourself buying a home at the peak of a housing boom and having to sell it when prices have declined, thereby leaving you with a much smaller down payment for your next home.

However, many employers reimburse transferred employees for expenses involved in selling and purchasing homes. Some employers will even make up the difference for any loss realized on the sale of a home. Thus, aside from the inconvenience of moving too often, such persons could benefit from home ownership.

Otherwise, for those willing to listen to dollar-and-cents reasoning, nothing can justify renting over owning in the long term. This remains true even if your purchase is a humble "starter home."

There are a number of ways of examining the rent/own question, some of which are exceptionally complex. Only two are looked at here and these only cursorily. First, let's assume that you will rent accommodation comparable to that which you would purchase, in which case all expenses in each situation will be identical. Ignoring the fact that your rent will continue to increase over the years, you are losing out in two important ways. First, a portion of your rent will, in all likelihood, go as profit to the owner of the rental property. It doesn't matter how much, but it does matter that there is some in every rent cheque. After all, the owner of the rental property would not be in the business of renting homes if he or she were not going to make a profit. Second, the owner of the rental property will realize the entire capital gain on the home when it is eventually sold. You, the tenant, get nothing when your lease is terminated.

If you owned this home, you would have an additional amount in your pocket each month representing the profit you otherwise would pay the owner of a rental property. Any accrued but unrealized capital gain on the home belongs to you. Thus, no matter what assumptions you make regarding rent, expenses, alternative investments or any other financial concept, you will always come out ahead when owning a home since, very simply, you are reaping the profit on rental and the capital gain that would otherwise go to the owner of the rental property.

A second, fairly straightforward way of examining the relative benefits of home ownership versus renting is to look at alternative investments. Again, let's make a few very general assumptions:

- You have exactly the same amount of cash invested in the home you own as does the rental property owner in a comparable home.
- The expenses for both homes are identical.
- The rental property owner does not realize any profit (an unrealistically conservative assumption) and therefore his rental income is the same as his expenses.

This means that you can rent or own comparable homes for exactly the same outlay each month, and therefore the only factor to examine is the amount you have invested in the home – that is, your accumulated equity. Given these factors, then, what return would you expect on the equity if you rented instead of owned? Or put another way, what kind of investment would you have to make to outperform investing in your own home?

The same figures used on page 57 are used again: namely, the house increases in value at a rate of 10% a year and inflation averages 7% annually. It is also assumed that you have been living for several years in your home, which you bought for $100,000. It is now worth $150,000 and you still have a mortgage of $75,000 on it. In other words, if you were to sell the house today and rent comparable accommodation, you would have $75,000 cash to invest. The rent you would then have to pay is exactly equal to the expenses you incurred while you owned the house.

In this situation, the after-tax real return for one year on the home you own is calculated as follows. The gain is 10% of $150,000, or $15,000. You have $75,000 equity in the home, the amount you otherwise would invest, and therefore your return on capital is 20% ($15,000/$75,000). The home is your principal residence so no tax will be payable if and when you sell it and realize the capital gain. Inflation is 7%, so your real gain is 13% (20% minus 7%).

If you sell the home and begin to rent, you would have $75,000 to invest. If you invested the money in interest-bearing securities, you would pay tax on all income earned at the rate of, say, 35% (it is assumed that you have already used up your $1,000 investment income deduction). Under these conditions, you would have to earn interest at almost 31% to realize an after-tax return of 20% and, if we assume an inflation rate of 7%, an after-tax *real* return of 13% on the $75,000. There are no such investments with reasonable security. If your return on investment consisted entirely of capital gains that were eligible for your $500,000 capital gains exemption, you would still have to realize a 20% return. Based on historical rates of return, this might be possible with an equity fund over the long term.

However, you should not forget the unrealistic assumptions that have been made regarding rent. In the real world, a large portion or perhaps all the earnings on the $75,000 would have to be used for the rental of comparable accommodation, leaving you with a much smaller, or perhaps no, return on your investment, whereas if you still owned the house, it would continue to appreciate at 10% each year.

Incidentally, the reason why first-time home-owners have so much less in their pockets than when they were renting is that, invariably, they have improved their accommodation. They have bought a larger, more luxurious and better located home.

You Should Have Bought a Home Last Year

The advice to all prospective home-purchasers is the same:

- Buy the best that you can comfortably afford.
- Buy location.
- Buy as soon as you can, even if it is not the house of your dreams.

Dreams change. That is why we have what the real estate industry calls *starter homes*. Most home-owners change homes several times, primarily because they want to improve the quality of the house and the location. The only reason most people are able to upgrade to a better quality home is because they bought one in the first place. They are able to trade up, using the equity built up in that first home.

What About a Condominium or Duplex?

The benefits described in this chapter regarding ownership of detached and semi-detached houses also apply to condominiums. Since you own the condominium, you also reap the benefits of any capital appreciation. However, since condominiums have been popular for only the past fifteen years or so, they have not been able to establish the investment track record of houses. Some have performed exceptionally well, increasing in value and holding the line on annual maintenance charges. Others have barely managed to sustain their original value or have seen the monthly fees zoom out of sight.

Condominiums are better than nothing and can be just as good an investment as a house – if you do your homework. Generally, you should only consider buying a condominium if the building is at least five years old. This will ensure that the builder or original purchasers have taken care of any serious faults in the building and that some kind of short-term track record has been established for the resale of units in the building or complex.

Many persons have purchased a duplex as their first home, living in part of the house while renting out the other part. When they can afford the mortgage payments themselves, they take over the whole house. There are a number of pros and cons to buying a duplex. Most certainly, it is not everyone's cup of tea.

Buying a duplex might allow you to begin home ownership earlier than you thought possible. The rental income generated from part of the house makes it easier to carry a mortgage, although you may have to put up a larger down payment. Nevertheless, you participate fully in the increase in the value of the house. In a few years, you will have the option of selling the house at a good profit or taking over the whole home while doing some renovations. Either way, you will probably be better off than if you had waited several more years to buy your first home.

If you buy a duplex, however, remember that you will have to be a landlord to the tenant who lives under your roof for a few years. Many people discover that being a landlord is one of the more unpleasant experiences of their lives and get rid of their tenants or the house as quickly as possible. Unfortunately, you probably will not discover how well or how poorly you adjust to being a landlord until you have been one for some time. As a landlord, you are running a business, the rental of real property, and must keep records and report income and expenses for tax purposes. You also may be subject to a variety of municipal laws as well as provincial landlord and tenant legislation, the bulk of which favours tenants. Perhaps most unsettling is the fact that you will put $10,000 or $20,000 down on the house and find that your living accommodations have not improved significantly. They may even have deteriorated if you have unpleasant tenants or have stretched your financial resources to the limit in order to buy. One of the points of the financial security formula is that it eliminates a great deal of worry. A duplex should provide close to or the same amount of physical enjoyment that a single-family house would. If you feel that there is any danger of a duplex proving to be a source of worry or misery, wait a year or two and buy a single-family house.

Saving for Your First Home – The Strategies

The elimination of RHOSPs (Registered Home Ownership Savings Plans) in the 1985 federal budget was a considerable blow to those saving for a first home. RHOSPs were the best tax shelter available to would-be home-buyers, and the only one that many lower income workers were ever likely to use. With a RHOSP, you received a tax deduction for contributing up to $1,000 a year, with a maximum of $10,000 over twenty years. Funds accumulated tax-free and you paid no tax on the funds if they were used to help buy an owner-occupied home.

Now you will have to use three of the five financial strategies to maximum advantage: first, the $1,000 investment income deduction; second, RRSPs; and third, if you are married, income splitting – which simply means that both you and your spouse make use of your respective $1,000 investment income deductions and RRSPs, thereby doubling up on the benefits. If approached properly, these three strategies should help provide you and your spouse with more than enough funds for a down payment on your first modestly priced home. In most urban areas, you will need no more than $20,000 to $25,000 to purchase a starter home with a 20% or 25% down payment. If both you and your spouse are working, it should not take long to accumulate this amount.

Remember the advice given at the beginning of this chapter? Buy as quickly as you can afford to. The sooner you are in a home of your own, the sooner you begin building up equity in that home, which means you'll be able to afford your dream home all that much sooner.

Planning Profile

A Toronto couple, David and Sarah Mancini, bought sooner than they really wanted to in mid-1985, acting on a real estate agent's advice that the lowest mortgage interest rate in a number of years would begin to push up the price of homes. They borrowed the extra $10,000 they needed from Sarah's parents, interest-free, for the first year. Shortly after they moved into their new home, the latest Toronto housing boom began. Eighteen months later, their house had increased in value by 50% to $150,000, which was still the average price of a home in the city. Sarah had just received a promotion, so they took out a larger mortgage and repaid the $10,000 to her parents.

A Toronto fairy tale, it's true, but similar price rises have been seen in most other major cities at some point, and it did indeed happen to tens of thousands of Toronto home-buyers in 1985-86.

So let's examine the strategies that you can use to buy your first home.

The $1,000 Investment Income Deduction

To accumulate funds for the purchase of a home, the first thing you should do is maximize your $1,000 investment income deduction each year.

If you earn interest income from Canadian sources or dividends from public Canadian companies, up to $1,000 of such income in total can be received tax-free each year. These amounts must be received at *arm's length*, which simply means that you cannot own a controlling interest in those companies that provide the income nor can you be closely related to someone who owns such a controlling interest in these companies.

Most types of interest from Canadian sources qualify for the deduction, including interest from banks or trust companies, as well as from bonds, mortgages and notes. Also, any Canadian-source interest you would include in income under the three-year accrual rules is eligible (see below).

The benefits of the $1,000 investment income deduction should not be underestimated. For example, you are much better off buying a $1,000 Canadian bond that pays interest at 10% than buying, say, a $1,000 bond (Canadian dollars) paying 12% issued by a company resident in the United States. Interest of $100 on the Canadian bond can be received free of tax if you have not used up your $1,000 investment income deduction, while tax of $36 is payable on the $120 interest (Canadian dollars) received on the U.S. bond (assuming a tax rate of 30%), leaving you with only $84 after taxes. In order to earn the same $100 after taxes as its Canadian counterpart, the U.S. bond would have to pay interest of more than 14% annually.

Money accumulates quickly when no tax is payable on the income earned by your invested funds. Assume, for example, that you put aside $1,400 of after-tax income ($2,000 of your pre-tax earnings minus tax at 30% of $600) at the beginning of each year to take advantage of the $1,000 deduction. At the end of five years, you will have $9,402 available for a down payment on your first home, assuming the funds earn 10% compounded annually.

Canadian Dividends   It is the *grossed-up amount,* or taxable amount, of dividends that is claimed under the $1,000 investment income deduction, not the actual cash amount. This taxable amount will appear on the T5 slip you receive from the payer of the dividend. Dividends from Canadian corporations are taxed at much lower rates than other types of income. The stock or shares of Canadian companies that pay dividends are not recommended as investments. However, you may indirectly receive such dividends if you invest in equity investment funds. The fund itself earns dividends. These might be flowed through to you each

65

year, in which case they must be reported in your income tax return.

The following example will explain how Canadian dividends are taxed and what amount is eligible for the $1,000 deduction.

Assume that you are taxed federally at 23% and that your provincial rate of tax is 50% of the federal rate. You receive a Canadian dividend of $900. For tax purposes, you gross this cash amount up by ⅓ or 33⅓% to $1,200 (before 1987, the gross-up was ½ or 50%). However, you now are eligible for the Dividend Tax Credit, which reduces the rate of tax you pay on the dividend. In theory, this process accounts for corporate tax already paid on the income out of which the corporation pays the dividend.

Cash dividend	$ 900
Add: Gross-up (33⅓% of $900)	300
Grossed-up or taxable dividend	$1,200
Tax at 23% on $1,200	$ 276
Less: Dividend tax credit equal to 16⅔% of grossed-up dividend	200
Net federal tax	76
Add: Provincial tax (50% of $76)	38
Total federal and provincial tax	$ 114

Total tax on this dividend is $114, which means the after-tax return is about 87% of your pre-tax return. If interest income of $900 were received, tax of about $310 would be payable, leaving you with an after-tax return of 65.5% of your pre-tax return.

In the above example, you would claim $1,000 of the grossed-up dividend of $1,200 under your $1,000 investment income deduction, even though you only received $900 cash. This may seem unfair if you have $100 of other Canadian investment income that is eligible for the deduction and you have to pay tax on it. However, note the net effect of claiming the dividend under your $1,000 investment income deduction: you must include the dividend in income, which produces a tax liability of $114. However, you can deduct $1,000 from income which, at a

34.5% combined federal and provincial marginal rate of tax, produces a $345 tax saving. In other words, you have received the $900 cash dividend and you are benefiting by an additional $231 ($345 minus $114). This in effect means that your after-tax return (dividend) on the Canadian shares is $1,131 ($900 plus $231).

If you had received the $900 in interest instead of dividends, the result would not be as advantageous. You would pay tax of $310 on the interest, and then claim the $900 under your $1,000 investment income deduction. This produces a $310 tax saving, so your after-tax return on the interest is the same as your pre-tax return – $900, but it is $231 less than the return on the dividend.

Unfortunately, dividend rates are usually considerably lower than interest rates on investments of similar risk for this very reason. Market forces tend to equalize the after-tax return for dividends and interest on investments of identical risk for individuals in the top tax bracket, although individuals in lower brackets may have somewhat of an advantage.

The taxable portion of capital gains realized on Canadian securities is no longer eligible for the $1,000 investment income deduction, now that the first $500,000 of capital gains is exempt from tax (see Chapter 9).

Deductible Interest Any interest expense incurred on funds borrowed to earn income qualifying for the $1,000 investment income deduction offsets this eligible income for purposes of the deduction (as explained in Chapter 3). For example, assume that you borrow $1,000 at 10% to buy a GIC which pays 10% interest. You pay interest of $100 on the loan and you receive $100 in interest from the GIC. The $100 interest expense is deductible from income and the $100 GIC interest qualifies for your $1,000 investment income deduction. However, you also must reduce the income qualifying for the $1,000 investment income deduction by the amount of the interest expense on the loan. Thus, the net effect is to deny you a tax exemption for the bond interest, but allow you a deduction for the interest expense. That is, you are prevented from getting a double deduction – once under your $1,000 investment income deduction, and again under the interest deductibility provisions.

Of course, in most situations, there would be no point in borrowing at 10% to earn 10% on the GICs.

Three-Year Accrual Rules You should be aware of the impact that the three-year accrual rules may have on your financial and investment planning. These rules essentially say that virtually all forms of interest income must be reported for tax purposes at least every three years, even if you have not received the income during that period. The rules also apply to certain annuities and life insurance policies. The rules prevent you from deferring income from taxation for extended periods of time.

For example, strips have become popular over the last couple of years. As you'll remember, these are simply the interest coupons stripped from long-term, high-quality, government-guaranteed bonds, which you buy at a discount. They increase in value each year you hold them, assuming that interest rates remain constant, and you can cash them for their face value upon maturity. The tax rules consider this increase in value each year as interest subject to the three-year accrual rules. Thus, if you buy strips outside your RRSP, you must report the increase in value at least every three years on your tax return and pay the appropriate amount of tax, even though you do not actually receive any cash. This will not prove to be a hardship if the interest on the strip can be exempted from tax under your $1,000 investment income deduction.

You have the option of electing to report deferred interest – that is, interest earned but not received – on any security annually instead of every three years. If you are not making full use of your $1,000 investment income deduction each year, you should make this election on some of your securities, since in the third year you may exceed your $1,000 limit. Bear in mind that you cannot carry forward any unused portion of the $1,000 deduction to a subsequent year.

Registered Retirement Savings Plans (RRSPs)

RRSPs are discussed in greater detail in Chapter 6 and Appendix B. Only a couple of the basic rules are summarized here. Under the new RRSP rules, which take effect beginning in 1988, you may contribute up to 18% of your earned income to an RRSP, to an annual maximum ($15,500 by 1991) which is deductible from income. However, if you are a member of a defined benefit pension plan, your RRSP contribution limit will be restricted depending on the contribution made to the company pension plan and the benefits that you are entitled to receive from that plan. If you belong to a money purchase pension plan, you may contribute up to the limit of 18% of earned income or $15,500, minus those contributions made by you and your employer to the money purchase plan. Company pension plans are discussed briefly on page 99.

In 1987, you may contribute up to 20% of your earned income to an RRSP to a maximum of $7,500. If you are a member of a company pension plan, your RRSP contribution is limited to a maximum of $3,500 minus deductible contributions you make to the company plan.

RRSPs act more like tax-sheltered investment vehicles than retirement savings plans, in that you can withdraw money from an RRSP whenever you want, as long as the withdrawal is brought into your income and is subject to tax. You receive a deduction for contributions to an RRSP, which means that your pre-tax earnings are invested. As well, no tax is payable as income is earned inside the RRSP.

If you institute an annual savings program, funds can accumulate quickly inside an RRSP. However, remember that tax must be paid on the RRSP funds withdrawn and used for a down payment on a home. For example, assume that you contribute $2,000 a year for five years to your RRSP and your marginal tax rate is 30%. At the end of five years, you will have accumulated $13,431 if you make your contribution at the beginning of each year and the RRSP earns 10% compounded annually. However, if the funds are withdrawn, you must include the amount in income and pay tax at your marginal rate. If your tax rate is still 30%, you will have $9,402 available for your home purchase.

As explained in Chapter 6, there is no tax on your net RRSP investment – that is,the amount you contribute to the RRSP, net of what you receive as a tax refund for making the contribution. In fact, you will notice that the $9,402 saved with the RRSP, after paying taxes, is exactly the same amount that is saved using the $1,000 investment income deduction.

Income Splitting

Everything a single person can do, a husband and wife can each do, thereby doubling their benefits. Each can contribute to his or her own RRSP, within the prescribed limits, and each has his or her own $1,000 investment income deduction.

Income splitting with a spouse is usually defined as having income, which would normally be taxed in the hands of the higher income spouse, earned by and taxed in the hands of the lower income spouse so that less tax or no tax is paid on that income. It can also be defined more generally as ensuring that there is as little difference as possible between the taxable incomes of each spouse. Splitting income with your spouse is sound financial advice that every married couple should take under consideration early in their working lives. You will improve your investment returns as a result of lowering the overall family tax liability, which consequently increases the funding available for purchasing your first home, as well as for achieving the other three fundamental financial goals.

Using the previous example in the context of the $1,000 investment income deduction, if both spouses save $1,400 of after-tax income each year for five years, the couple will accumulate almost $19,000, which could be enough for a down payment on a first home.

The other major objective of income splitting is to ensure that if one spouse temporarily leaves the work force, he or she continues to earn as much as possible during this time, rather than one spouse earning all the income. This should lower the total tax bill of both spouses. Again, the secret to accomplishing this is to begin planning now, particularly if you are relatively young and both of you are working. Generally, you will arrange for the spouse who is expected to temporarily leave the work force to begin immediately earning the greater part of the couple's investment income. This income will be taxed more lightly now since some of it is being earned by the lower income spouse instead of the higher income spouse. And when the lower income spouse is no longer earning work-related income, the investment income may escape tax entirely. The benefits of income splitting, as well as several income splitting techniques, are discussed in more detail in Chapter 9.

Which Investments to Use When Saving for Your First Home

You should be planning to purchase your first home as quickly as possible, so it is fairly safe to assume that only a few years will elapse between the time you begin a serious savings program and the date of purchase. If both you and your spouse are earning income from full-time work, it may only take two or three years to accumulate a substantial down payment. Thus, you should be looking at shorter-term investments that offer the greatest protection for your invested capital.

In most cases, however, you won't know in advance when you will have accumulated enough funds, and you never know when a suitable house may come up for sale. Thus, you cannot pick a specific term over which to invest. If you lock $4,000 into a five-year GIC, these funds will not do you much good if you decide to buy your house in two years. So you will need flexible investments that can be liquidated on relatively short notice.

Canada Savings Bonds (CSBs), T-Bills, money market income investment funds, term deposits and high-interest savings accounts all work well in this situation. You should steer clear of equity funds or other income investment funds, since they are strictly long-term investments. With only a two- or three-year investment horizon, you may buy into an equity investment fund at the peak of the market cycle and actually find that you have lost money when the time comes to redeem your units in the fund to buy your home. You should also avoid strips and GICs, as they are longer-term investments.

Maximize Your $1,000 Investment Income Deduction First, you and your spouse should each maximize your $1,000 investment income deductions. With your first $5,000 (each spouse), buy Canada Savings Bonds. CSBs provide a good, secure return and you can cash them at any time to finance the down payment on your first home. It is likely that you will buy that home sooner than you think. Unfortunately, you have to wait until about the end of October each year to purchase CSBs. While waiting, put your funds into a money market fund each month if possible, or a high-interest savings account. If you can accumulate larger amounts quickly, you could also put your cash into higher-interest T-bills or deposit receipts that mature shortly before November.

With the remaining portion of your $1,000 investment income deduction (each spouse), buy 90- or 180-day T-Bills. These may pay slightly more interest than CSBs. If interest rates go up, you will be able to take advantage of the higher rates when you renew your T-Bills. If interest rates fall, your CSBs will continue to pay their higher rate at least until the next November. You could also consider investing in a money market fund instead of T-Bills.

If you decide to buy a home on short notice, you can cash the CSBs and sell your T-Bills and units in the money market fund almost instantly. You receive the face value of the CSBs plus interest accumulated to the end of the preceding month. With T-Bills, you receive interest at current market rates.

Bear in mind that you may be earning other interest income, probably from the savings or chequing account that you use for day-to-day expenses. This also must be included in your tax return and is exempt under your $1,000 investment income deduction.

If you plan to purchase a home within two or three years, looking for an interest rate that is a percentage point or two higher than that available on CSBs or T-Bills may not be enough incentive to opt for what will probably be a less flexible investment. For example, if you save $4,000 at the beginning of each year for two years, you will accumulate only $128 more at 10% than you would at 9% compounded annually. If 11% is earned instead of 9%, the difference is $256 at the end of two years.

However, if buying a home is definitely not in your immediate plans, by all means take advantage of the higher interest rates available with GICs.

Contribute to an RRSP Once you have maximized your $1,000 investment income deduction, you can start to use RRSPs to fund the rest of the down payment needed for the purchase of your first home. If you are single, you might need to accumulate another 15% to 20% of the purchase price of the home in the RRSP. If you are married, you might already have enough funds, or both of you will, in total, need to accumulate only about 5% to 10% more, which probably will result in relatively small RRSP contributions.

If you are considering an RRSP, you are probably close now to making a decision on a home and do not want your funds tied up in any particular investment for longer than thirty to sixty days. An RRSP money market fund is ideal at this time, but you might shop around for a high-interest savings account type of RRSP into which you (both spouses) will put your savings.

If you are married, the lower income spouse should consider contributing to the RRSP before the higher income spouse to get your income splitting program off on the right foot. With any luck the RRSP contributions made by the lower income spouse will still be in the RRSP in forty or fifty years and will have increased in value a hundred times or more.

Getting Ready to Take the Plunge

You have saved up the down payment – now comes the payoff. Unfortunately, purchasing a home is a bit more complicated than buying the week's groceries. There are a hundred and one things to consider and traps to avoid, all but one of which is beyond the scope of this book. The first thing you should do is talk to friends who own a home, preferably those who have recently purchased the same type of home in which you are interested. They are your best and most reliable source of information. Next, shop around for a suitable agent. It may take you a day to buy a home or it may take six months, which is a long time to be dealing with someone you do not like. Finally, get a firm idea of what you want and set your sights at a reasonable level. This is usually possible only after you have looked at a number of homes for sale, sometimes dozens.

Shopping for a Mortgage

The type of mortgage that you should get on your first home will very much depend on your particular situation – and there are hundreds of choices. Try to begin shopping for the mortgage that suits you best at about the time that you begin looking for the house. The mortgage you choose should allow you to make payments as large as you can comfortably afford and allow you to pay off significant amounts of principal periodically. What may seem like a back-breaking amount to pay each month now will hardly be noticed in five years, assuming you have taken out a five-year mortgage. Your payments will generally be exactly the same, but there is every possibility that your family income will have more than doubled as a result of salary increases and promotions.

What term of mortgage to get? The longer the term, the better you can arrange your financial affairs, since you know that a specific amount is due on the mortgage at the first of each month for the next four or five, or even six or seven years. But locking yourself into a five-year mortgage when interest rates are dropping is not a wise decision. Historically, five-year mortgage interest rates have ranged from two to five percentage points above the inflation rate. If current rates are within or below this range and inflation is relatively low, from an historical perspective, it is probably safe to take out a long-term mortgage. If the current five-year rate is above this range, you should probably consider a shorter-term mortgage or a variable rate mortgage that can be locked into a five-year term at your option. If the inflation rate shows any sign of heading toward the double-digit range, you should consider locking in a long-term mortgage as quickly as possible.

Bear in mind that more principal will have been paid down on a long-term mortgage than on a short-term one when the time comes to renew. This can be extremely important if interest rates have rocketed out of sight, since payments on the renewed smaller mortgage may at least be in the same ball park as your old payments, despite the higher interest rate on the renewed mortgage.

What About Paying Down the Mortgage?

Paying down the outstanding principal on a mortgage is one of the better investments a home-owner can make, as you will see in Step 4 of the financial security formula. Notice, however, that it is ranked after contributing towards your retirement with RRSPs, which, unless you are close to retirement age, will be a better investment than paying down the mortgage.

Should You Use the $1,000 Investment Income Deduction or an RRSP to Save for the Down Payment on Your First Home?

As you will recall from the examples on pages 65 and 69, exactly the same amount, $9,402, is available using either the $1,000 investment income deduction or an RRSP. You contributed $2,000 to the RRSP, but your taxes were reduced by $600 (tax rate of 30% times $2,000). Thus, your net investment in the RRSP (investment after tax) is $1,400 ($2,000 minus $600), the same amount invested in respect of your $1,000 investment income deduction. Thus, you do not, in effect, pay tax on your net investment in an RRSP if your tax rate is the same when you withdraw the funds as when you made the contribution to the RRSP.

Therefore, when saving for a home, should you use an RRSP or the $1,000 investment income deduction? And if using both, which should you use first?

The safest course to follow is to maximize your $1,000 investment income deduction first and then contribute to the RRSP. There are several reasons why.

First, if your tax rate has increased by the time you withdraw funds from your RRSP for the home purchase, which is often the case, you will be left with less cash than if you used your $1,000 investment income deduction each year. Using the numbers in the example above, except that your tax rate after five years is 40% instead of 30%, you will be left with only $8,059 using the RRSP, whereas you would still have $9,402 using the $1,000 investment income deduction.

If your tax rate happens to drop, you would be better off with the RRSP. It is highly unlikely that a working person's marginal tax rate will decline; and if it does, you probably would not be in a position to buy a house since your income will have dropped fairly significantly. As might be expected, there is an exception to this general observation (see below).

Second, you can still use the funds invested in respect of the

$1,000 investment income deduction as an RRSP contribution after 1988 if you later decide not to buy the home, or if the money for the down payment comes from another source. Before 1988, it is not possible to catch up on RRSP contributions not made in a particular year, so it is important that you maximize your RRSP contributions each year. Beginning in 1989, you will be allowed to make up for RRSP contributions that you were permitted to make but did not make in years after 1987. Beginning in 1995, this catch-up period will be restricted to the previous seven years. If you can make an RRSP contribution equivalent to everything invested in respect of the $1,000 investment income deduction, plus all earnings, plus the amount of any tax reduction that results from making the RRSP contribution, you will be in the same position as if you had not contributed to the RRSP in each previous year.

This RRSP catch-up provision also will allow you to ensure that investment income does not become taxable. As soon as you are about to earn more than the tax-exempt $1,000, you would make an appropriate contribution to your RRSP where the earnings should not be subject to any tax.

Third, by first maximizing your $1,000 investment income deduction, you avoid any RRSP fees, although these are usually minimal for savings account and money market fund RRSPs earning only interest income.

There is one situation, however, where it may be prudent to use an RRSP before your $1,000 investment income deduction. Sometimes one spouse will temporarily drop out of the work force at the time the house is purchased, in which case this spouse's tax rate will probably decline. In this situation, you may be much better off using the RRSP than the $1,000 investment income deduction. For example, assume that the person in the above example has no income in the year the home is purchased. You cash in the RRSP, which means you must include the entire $13,431 accumulated in the RRSP in income for tax purposes. Using 1987 tax rates (provincial tax is 50% of federal tax), you will be left with over $11,000 after paying taxes, which is a substantial increase over the $9,402 accumulated if you use the $1,000 investment income deduction.

If You Have Amounts in an RRSP, Should You Use Them as a Down Payment on Your First Home?

The answer is a qualified yes – but only if you see no other possible way of financing the purchase of your first home within the next two years or so. Home ownership is a higher financial priority than investing in an RRSP, although not in every case a better investment.

Planning Profile

Bill and Lucy Walchuk, a Halifax couple in their mid-twenties already have about $24,000 accumulated exclusively in Lucy's RRSP, where it is earning about 15% a year since it is invested in equity investment funds. If they do not buy a home, it is likely this amount could remain intact for up to thirty-five or forty years, when it will finally be used to produce a retirement income.

They also have the option of cashing in the RRSP and using the proceeds, which they estimate will amount to about $20,000, as a down payment on an $85,000 home.

If they do not buy the home, the RRSP will be worth almost $400,000 in twenty years. If they do buy the home and it appreciates in value at 8% annually, the house will be worth almost the same amount after twenty years – $400,000. Bear in mind, however, that if they sell the house, they would not be taxable on the gain, whereas the full amount in the RRSP is taxable.

And, by buying the home, they no longer pay rent, which will constantly escalate over the following twenty years. In fact, by purchasing the home, a considerable amount of cash will eventually be freed up each year – cash that can be used for investment purposes. The amount of cash depends on how fast they discharge their mortgage. But, if they manage to pay it off in ten years, they will be able to add at least $170,000 to their net worth in the succeeding ten years, for a total amount of about $570,000, which is considerably more than is in the RRSP (assuming they can earn an after-tax return of about 15% over the ten-year period.)

In Bill and Lucy's case, the home appears to be a better investment than the RRSP, assuming the future unfolds as expected. Still, if you have funds in an RRSP, you should first try other methods of accumulating a down payment before you give up the benefit that compounding will produce if the funds are left intact in the RRSP over extended periods. One solution is to borrow from relatives. If you can repay the loan at a reasonable interest rate within five or six years of acquiring the home, you will have both the home and the RRSP, and be that much better off.

Should You Use Your Emergency Fund as a Down Payment on Your First Home?

As discussed earlier, setting up a special emergency fund receives a low priority ranking in the financial security formula. In fact, you should consider using any emergency fund you may have – first as a down payment on a home, second as an RRSP contribution, and third to pay down the mortgage on your home. Only then should you consider building up an emergency fund.

The question, then, is who is better off – the couple with the house, or the couple with the emergency fund? Consider the following case.

Planning Profile

A Winnipeg couple, Ernesto and Pamela Ciprianno, bought a home four years ago for $50,000 using their emergency fund of $10,000 as a down payment. They took out a $40,000 mortgage. The house is now worth about $70,000 (an 8% gain each year), and they have reduced their mortgage to about $37,000, giving them a net equity in the home of $33,000 ($70,000 minus $37,000).

An emergency of some sort arises that requires the expenditure of $15,000 over the next year. Ernesto and Pamela have little ready cash, so they raise a new, higher mortgage on their home to finance the emergency. They increase their mortgage by $17,000 and use $15,000 for the emergency. The other $2,000 is used to pay the higher mortgage payments during the year.

At the end of the year, their home is worth $75,600 (an 8% gain over the year), and they have a mortgage of about $54,000. Their equity in their home has been reduced to about $21,600 ($75,600 minus $54,000), which is $11,400 less than their equity at the beginning of the year ($33,000 minus $21,600).

If the Cipriannos had not bought the house, their emergency fund would have grown to about $15,000 after four years (assuming an 11% earnings rate after taxes, compounded annually). Their entire fund would have been used for the emergency and at the end of the fifth year, they would have had to start saving all over again. There is no doubt that they are better off having bought the home.

There are two caveats to this story. First, if the emergency happens the day after Ernesto and Pamela buy their home, they will be in worse shape than if they had kept their emergency fund intact. They will not be able to raise a larger mortgage and would probably have to sell the house at a loss because of real estate fees. Only after about two years will they be better off with the house.

Second, if they do not become home-owners, they probably would live in accommodation that is inferior and less expensive than the home they purchased, and therefore they might have a larger emergency fund available. But even if the fund tripled in size to, say, $30,000, they would still be better off with the house. They have a $21,600 equity in their home after five years compared to about $16,500 that would be left over after the emergency if they had not bought the home ($15,000 plus one year's earnings).

6
Third Step: Get the Most from Your RRSP

It is notoriously difficult to convince someone in their twenties to think about saving for retirement, let alone to do anything positive about it. If you are single or newly married, your attention probably is directed more to buying your first home and with good reason. Also, if you have already bought your first home and have children, you are likely more concerned with upgrading your lifestyle and funding your children's education. Yet the best time to begin a retirement savings program is when you are in your twenties. If you need proof, consider that if the RRSP earns 10% compounded annually and if you contribute $1,000 a year to an RRSP from age twenty-five to age thirty-one, you will have about as much retirement income at age sixty-five as someone who contributes $1,000 a year to an RRSP every year from age thirty-two to sixty-four. That's seven years of contributing compared to thirty-three! Once again, the magic of compounding rears its wondrous head.

Saving for retirement or, more specifically, contributing to RRSPs, is ranked third in the financial security formula for a variety of reasons, not the least of which are the long-term benefits that can arise if you begin a savings program early in your career. From an emotional point of view, establishing an emergency fund or saving for your children's college education might rank at the top of your financial priorities, but from a dollar-and-cents perspective, putting as much as possible into RRSPs makes the most sense. The government helps you save for retirement by providing substantial tax savings, whereas no such assistance is available if you are simply putting money aside for your children's college tuition. When children are finally of college age, many families discover that they can, for the most part, fund their children's education needs from current earnings. If they cannot, RRSPs are flexible enough that a portion of this retirement savings can be used for educational purposes if absolutely necessary.

Three Cornerstones of Retirement Saving

For the average Canadian, there are three cornerstones to successfully saving for retirement:

1. Ensuring that you collect any government retirement pensions that are available.
2. Paying off the mortgage on your home.
3. Maximizing retirement saving, whether in the form of RRSPs and/or company pension plans or profit-sharing plans.

If you adhere to these principles throughout the twenty-five or thirty years leading up to retirement, you might find that you are actually better off when you retire than when you were in the work force.

Government Pensions You have virtually no control over your contributions to the Canada Pension Plan, nor the benefits to which you will eventually become entitled. In fact, it might be safer to assume that the benefits from the Canada Pension Plan and Old Age Security will not be as attractive in ten or twenty years as they are now. No one should be depending on them to provide a significant portion of their retirement income.

Mortgage-Free Home Paying down your mortgage and eventually owning a debt-free home is Step 4 in the financial security formula and the subject of the next chapter.

Private Retirement Saving There are three categories of private saving:

1. Employer-sponsored Registered Pension Plans (RPPs) or Deferred Profit-Sharing Plans (DPSPs);
2. RRSPs (Registered Retirement Savings Plans); and
3. Private, non-tax-assisted saving.

The average employee has little control over his or her contributions or the employer's contributions to an RPP or DPSP, or over the pension benefits that will eventually be received. RPPs and DPSPs are discussed briefly at the end of this chapter and in Appendix B in the context of pension reform.

Non-tax-assisted saving – or, more simply, private investing – is covered by Step 5 and Step 6 in the financial security formula and is the subject of Chapters 8 and 9. People invest with a variety of goals in mind, but investing to eventually generate additional retirement income should come first. Once you retire, you will probably have no way to generate new income, and any extra you can begin earning now will be appreciated.

The bulk of this chapter deals with retirement saving through RRSPs, the second-best investment the average Canadian will make in his or her lifetime.

Registered Retirement Savings Plans (RRSPs)

Over the course of this chapter, it will be more helpful to look upon RRSPs as tax-assisted investment vehicles – that is, you contribute funds to an RRSP and these funds are then invested. Nevertheless, a variety of investments, such as GICs or eligible investment funds, can be registered as RRSP investments. Most people think of an RRSP this way and refer to them as investments, this author included. However, eventually you should open a self-directed RRSP, to which you will normally make cash contributions and then direct how that cash is invested, within the tax rules governing RRSPs. Actually, an RRSP itself is nothing more than a contract between you and a financial institution (in this case, called the RRSP administrator or issuer). Under this contract, the issuer agrees to treat any contributions according to the RRSP tax rules.

RRSPs are attractive for a variety of reasons:

- You are allowed to contribute pre-tax dollars to the RRSP, and earnings in the RRSP are not taxed. Only when you withdraw funds from the RRSP, either as retirement income or as a lump sum, are you taxed on everything received.
- They are extremely flexible. You can cash in all or a portion of your RRSP at any time, although you must include the amount in income for tax purposes. The funds do not have to be used to provide you with a

retirement income. Or you can hang on to the RRSP until age seventy-one and then begin receiving a retirement income.

- They are extremely accessible. In January and February of each year, everybody seems to be selling RRSPs in every shape and size. You can even make a contribution by phone. For the average Canadian worker, the RRSP contribution rules and available investment options are relatively straightforward and can be dealt with quickly once a year. You can open up a savings account RRSP where you bank, or your broker can establish a self-directed plan in which you are responsible for making the investment decisions. Qualifying investments range from savings accounts to listed stock options to your own mortgage. Not entirely by accident, the eight investments recommended in the financial security formula also qualify.
- RRSPs are flexible on retirement. Retirement incomes can be arranged to suit virtually every need.
- The tax-saving advantages of RRSPs are nothing short of spectacular. In fact, RRSPs actually eliminate tax on your net investment (see below). The tax shelter aspect even continues into retirement, since only amounts actually received as RRSP retirement income each year are taxed, leaving the remainder tax-sheltered. In addition, you become entitled to the $1,000 pension deduction and the old age deduction once you reach the age of sixty-five, which can act to reduce the tax levied on RRSP retirement income.
- It is possible that your marginal tax rate will be higher when you contribute to the RRSP than when you receive retirement income from it, which provides you with a further tax saving.
- Spousal RRSPs provide an easy way to split income with your spouse, which reduces the combined tax bill of you and your spouse during retirement.
- For many Canadians, RRSPs are the only tax-assisted retirement savings vehicle to which they will have access. They shouldn't be ignored.

Table 6.1: Annual Retirement Income Generated With and Without RRSP

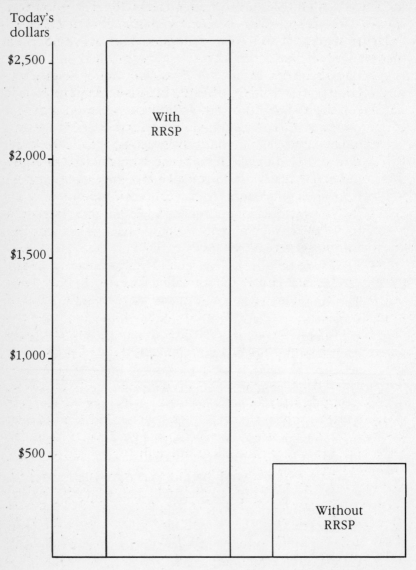

Today's dollars

Assumes $5,000 of pre-tax income ($3,250 of after-tax income) is invested for forty years at 10% compounded annually, and inflation rate of 6% annually

How Good Are RRSPs? Let's look at an example. If $5,000 is contributed to an RRSP today, it grows to over $226,000 in forty years if income is earned at 10% compounded annually. If inflation averages 6% over that period, you would accumulate about $22,000 in today's dollars, which will buy an annual, taxable retirement income (annuity) of about $2,600 in today's dollars.

If you invested outside an RRSP, you would not be nearly as well off. First, less could be invested because tax would have to be paid on the $5,000. Your $5,000 RRSP contribution consisted of after-tax cash of $3,250 plus your tax refund of $1,750 (assuming tax at a rate of 35% on $5,000). By investing outside the RRSP, you do not receive the tax refund because no amount is deductible from income, and therefore only $3,250 is available to invest.

Second, the income earned each year outside the RRSP might be taxed. Thus, on your investment of $3,250, your after-tax rate of return each year could be only 6.5% (65% of 10%). At this rate, you would accumulate only about $40,000, or about $3,900 in today's dollars at the end of forty years. This will buy an annual retirement income in today's dollars of about $460, only a portion of which would be taxable. With the RRSP, you are better off from a before-tax perspective by about $2,140, an improvement of over 500%. So if you have the means, there is no excuse for not making the maximum contribution to an RRSP each year.

No Tax on Net RRSP Investment An astute financial writer pointed out not too long ago that RRSPs are the perfect tax shelter since you never pay a dime of income tax on your net RRSP investment. Yes, you do pay tax when you collapse your RRSP or receive a retirement income, but the government finances your tax bill by means of its original contribution to your plan – your tax saving. Assume you contribute the $5,000 to an RRSP and your marginal tax rate is 35%. In effect, what you do is put up $3,250 of your own after-tax cash, and the government puts up the other $1,750 by allowing you a tax deduction of $5,000 and the consequent reduction in tax payable of $1,750. Assuming your marginal tax rate remains at 35%, you will eventually receive all income earned on your $3,250 net RRSP contribution (plus the original $3,250) tax-free, while the income earned on the government's $1,750 contribution plus the $1,750 is devoted entirely to taxes payable on your total RRSP income. In other words, you never pay tax on your net RRSP investment.

Assume that you collapse your $5,000 RRSP after one year and pay the required tax at 35%. You will have accumulated $5,500 if the RRSP earns 10%. Since you must pay tax of $1,925, this leaves you with $3,575. If you were to earn 10% outside your RRSP on your after-tax cash amount of $3,250 over one year, this would grow to $3,575 assuming no tax is payable – the same amount you receive from your RRSP after paying tax. Bear in mind, however, that tax might be payable on the income earned outside the RRSP.

Table 6.2: Why You Pay No Tax on Your Net RRSP Investment

	Inside RRSP	Outside RRSP
After-tax Income (Net RRSP investment)	$3,250	$3,250
Add: Tax Saving	1,750	—
Total Amount Invested (contributed to RRSP)	5,000	3,250
Add: Earnings for One Year at 10%	500	325
Total Before Tax	5,500	3,575
Less: Tax Payable at 35%	1,925	—
	$3,575	$3,575

- $5,000 contributed for one year (net investment – $3,250)
- $3,250 invested outside RRSP – no tax on earnings

This example assumes that when you collapse the RRSP your tax rate is the same as when you initially made the contribution. If your tax rate goes up, you will eventually pay a small amount of tax on your net investment. However, if your tax rate declines, you (not the government) will receive some of the income earned on the tax refund portion of your RRSP contribution. In this situation, the government, in effect, pays you for making the RRSP contribution.

Basic Rules for Contributing to an RRSP

The new RRSP rules introduced with pension reform will take effect on January 1, 1988, although a number of provisions, such as those regarding contribution limits, will be phased in over the next few years. However, other than the overhaul of the contribution mechanism and the new seven-year carry-forward provision, only a few minor changes have been made to the RRSP rules. The basic rules for 1987 contributions, as well as those for 1988 and following years are summarized only briefly here, although they are explored in more detail in Appendix B.

Limits are imposed on the amount you can contribute to an RRSP each year and deduct from income. In 1987, the standard limit is 20% of earned income to a maximum of $7,500. If you are a member of a company-sponsored Registered Pension Plan (RPP) or a Deferred Profit-Sharing Plan (DPSP), the limit is 20% of earned income to a maximum of $3,500 minus your contributions to the RPP.

Beginning in 1988, the standard limit is the lesser of 18% of earned income in the immediately preceding year and a specific dollar amount which is phased in as follows:

1988	$9,500
1989	$11,500
1990	$13,500
1991	$15,500

Thus, if you are subject to the 18% limit in 1988, your RRSP contribution will be based on your earned income in 1987, and you will be allowed to contribute a maximum of $9,500.

Earned income generally includes employment income (after deducting the $500 employment expense deduction), net business income, net rental income, alimony or maintenance receipts, royalties received by authors or inventors, net research grants and pension benefits. Beginning in 1988, amounts paid as alimony or maintenance are deducted when determining earned income and, beginning in 1990, pension benefits will no longer be included.

If you are a member of a *money purchase* RPP or a DPSP, your RRSP limit is reduced by all amounts contributed by you and/or your employer to either plan and deducted from income.

If you are a member of a *defined benefit* pension plan, your RRSP limit is reduced by an amount that is based on the benefits available from the RPP, less $600. This amount depends on the particular plan to which you belong. For example, assume that your earned income is $35,000 and your company-sponsored defined benefit RPP will pay pension benefits that are 60% of the maximum allowed (few plans pay the maximum). Your RRSP contribution limit is $6,300 (18% of $35,000). However, this is reduced by $3,180, calculated as 60% of $6,300 minus $600. Thus, you are allowed to contribute $3,120 ($6,300 minus $3,180) to your RRSP.

One of the significant pension reform proposals for RRSPs is the seven-year carry-forward provision, which begins in 1989 in respect of a carry forward from the 1988 tax year. The carry-forward mechanism will be fully implemented by 1995. In any year that you do not make a maximum contribution to your RRSP, you may carry forward this unused *contribution room* for seven years. For example, assume that you could have contributed $5,000 in 1988, but you contributed only $3,000. In any year up to and including 1995, the seventh year following 1988, you may contribute the $2,000 you failed to contribute in 1988 and receive a tax deduction for the contribution.

Before the end of each year beginning in 1988, you will be informed by the government of your total accumulated RRSP contribution room.

Contributions made to an RRSP during the first sixty days of a year are deductible in either that year or the previous year.

Relatively severe penalties apply if you contribute more than your maximum dollar limit to your RRSP. Penalties also apply if you have non-qualified investments in your self-directed RRSP. The most common non-qualified investments are shares in a private company with which you do not deal at arm's length. Also, you are allowed to invest in foreign securities only to a maximum of 10% of the cost of total investments in the particular RRSP, although you will be allowed to invest an additional $3 in foreign securities for every $1 invested in eligible Canadian small businesses. Investments in foreign securities can only be made through a self-directed RRSP, although many RRSP-eligible investment funds have up to 10% of their assets invested abroad.

RRSPs are available at banks, trust companies, credit unions and *caisses populaires*, as well as from insurance companies and stockbrokers. In many cases, you can also purchase units in an RRSP-eligible investment fund directly from the fund itself.

You can transfer your RRSP funds from one plan to another, providing it is done directly and you do not personally receive the funds. You might do this if one financial institution was offering a better return on your money, or you wanted to switch to a better-managed RRSP fund to improve your return. If you do withdraw funds from an RRSP and receive the funds directly, they are included in income in that year and are subject to tax. Remember that you can have as many different RRSP plans as you desire.

Finally, if you borrow money to make an RRSP contribution, remember that you are not allowed to deduct the interest paid on the borrowed funds from income for tax purposes.

RRSP Retirement Options Upon retirement you will have a variety of RRSP retirement income options from which to choose, including life and fixed-term annuities and Registered Retirement Income Funds (RRIFs). Choosing the most suitable package is extremely important and should not be left to the last minute. RRSPs must be converted to retirement income on or before December 31 of the year in which you reach the age of seventy-one. Otherwise the entire RRSP may be included in your income for tax purposes, or the institution holding your RRSP may convert it into a retirement income that does not meet your needs. A number of quality publications deal with RRSP retirement options. If the amounts in your RRSP are significant, it may be worthwhile getting professional advice.

Investing with Your RRSP

As noted earlier, an RRSP can be regarded as a vehicle for investing. You can buy a GIC where you bank and choose whether or not to have it registered as an RRSP investment. And, as you'll see later in this chapter, you can also open a self-directed RRSP, contribute cash to the plan and make your own investment decisions with that cash.

A wide variety of investments qualify for RRSPs, including the eight basic investments (investment funds must specifically qualify, which means their assets must be limited to certain investments). However, not all eight are suitable RRSP investments and several can usually be purchased only with a self-directed RRSP.

In general, you should make RRSP investments with the long term in mind. After all, these are funds you do not intend to use until your retirement years. However, RRSPs are also extremely flexible. You can liquidate your RRSP investments at any time, bearing in mind restrictions that might be placed on specific investments, and use the cash either for emergencies or to help with your children's education. Unfortunately, tax will probably be payable since such amounts must be included in your tax return for that year. In most cases, then, you will want several different types of RRSP investments.

Another reason for having a variety of different RRSP investments is that your investment goals will change as you grow older. When you are relatively young, for example, your primary goal is to accumulate as much as possible in the RRSP by maximizing earnings so that as much retirement income as possible will eventually be available. However, the closer you get to retirement, the more concerned you will be with protecting your accumulated wealth so that the expected amount of retirement income will indeed be available. This means reducing your level of investment risk and, consequently, accepting a smaller return on your investments.

Therefore, in terms of the eight basic investments, you will concentrate on equity investment funds when you are younger, since over the long term they should perform better than interest-bearing investments. In addition, you should set aside a small amount for quick withdrawal from the RRSP if it becomes necessary. As you approach retirement age, you will shift your focus to interest-bearing investments, since they offer better protection for your capital than equities.

The type of RRSP investment you make will also depend on the total value of RRSP contributions made by you and your spouse. Here is a rough breakdown of how you might invest as the value of your RRSP increases.

$0-$5,000 It is best to treat the first $5,000 you contribute to RRSPs as the flexible, short-term portion. Canada Savings Bonds or T-Bills would be ideal investments, but these are usually only available through a self-directed plan, which you may choose to set up later when you have contributed at least $20,000 to RRSPs. The best place to put your first $5,000 is in a money market investment fund or a high-interest savings account – preferably the type that pays a premium rate if you keep a minimum balance of, say, $5,000. Money market funds are more flexible since you can contribute much smaller amounts and still earn an attractive rate of interest.

$5,000-$20,000 You now begin investing in equity funds. It is suggested that you put $5,000 in each of three different funds. In addition to spreading your risk to some extent, this will also allow you to diversify among funds that have different investment goals. For instance, one fund may be dedicated to investing aggressively by picking only those stocks that promise high capital appreciation over the short term. Another may invest only in secure blue chip shares that will increase in value over the long term but will also pay dividends. A third fund may invest in out-of-favour, undervalued companies or perhaps invest in specific industry sectors. There are hundreds of equity funds available, each with different track records and varying styles of management. Since more of your income will eventually be invested in equity funds than in all the other investments combined, you should plan on doing a little bit of homework to find the funds that reflect your needs.

$20,000-$25,000 You might consider a portfolio mix of 75% equities and 25% interest-bearing investments when you are relatively young, although it will not hurt to have an even higher percentage in equity funds. Remember that your home – a secure, conservative investment – is also increasing in value and can be looked upon in the same light as an interest-bearing security.

You should invest the next $5,000 contribution to your RRSP in

91

strips or in an income investment fund, both of which are long-term, interest-bearing investments. There are dozens of income funds around, many of which have had very impressive track records over the past few years. Bond funds in particular have prospered because of the large drop in interest rates between 1982 and 1986. Again, plan on doing some homework to find the best fund. At least one trust company offers strips as a direct RRSP investment, but generally they must be purchased through a self-directed plan.

$25,000-$40,000 You can now begin repeating investment steps. This next $15,000 also goes into equity funds. You can simply use the same three funds or you might choose to add a fourth or a fifth fund to your RRSP portfolio.

Self-Directed RRSPs

Once you have contributed $20,000 or $25,000 to an RRSP, you should seriously consider opening a self-directed plan. There are at least three specific advantages to this type of RRSP.

First, periodic reporting on your investments will be consolidated on one statement, usually issued monthly, which will allow you to keep better track of your investments. For example, you might now have five separate RRSPs and possibly more. It is not uncommon to have more than a dozen different RRSPs purchased from a variety of institutions. Arranging to have all your RRSPs transferred to a self-directed plan is a simple matter. An annual fee is charged by the administrator of the self-directed plan, which can range from $50 for discount brokers, to $100 for full service brokers. Some trust companies may charge several hundred dollars, although additional services are included in this fee.

Second, a self-directed plan gives you more investing flexibility. You can acquire Canada Savings Bonds, T-Bills and strips in your self-directed plan, as well as the other investments, including investment funds. As a result, you should improve the overall return on your RRSPs, which will more than make up for the annual administrative fee.

Third, with a self-directed plan, you can take advantage of the rule that allows you to invest up to 10% of the cost of your RRSP investments in foreign securities. Thus, if your self-directed plan includes $5,000 in CSBs, $15,000 in RRSP-eligible equity funds and $5,000 in an RRSP-eligible income fund, you could put as much as $2,500 into an equity fund that invests primarily in non-Canadian securities. It is suggested that you invest your 10% in an international equity fund, whose investments are not restricted to the shares of companies in just one country. Several of these funds have extremely impressive long-term track records, performing much better than those RRSP-eligible funds that invest primarily in Canadian shares.

With a self-directed RRSP, you should split the interest-bearing portion of your portfolio between income investment funds and strips, except for the first $5,000, which could be invested in T-Bills or a money market fund.

A Word about Long-Term Interest Rates When you are considering buying interest-bearing investments, you should pay some attention to the expected movement of long-term interest rates. If you feel that rates are particularly low and should move higher in the near future, buy short-term instruments such as T-Bills or CSBs. If you feel rates are exceptionally high and will probably fall in the near future, buy long-term strips. In fact, you might want to use some of your equity fund contributions to buy such strips at this point, and when rates are lower, buy equity funds with contribution cash that would have been used to acquire interest-bearing securities.

If interest rates seem to be relatively low and show no sign of moving up or down, examine the real return available from interest-bearing securities. If inflation is running at 4% and strips are paying 10%, your real return is 6%. Real returns on interest-bearing investments have traditionally been between 2% and 4% above the inflation rate. Thus, a 6% real return should be considered attractive. If the real return were only average – say, 3% – you might consider short-term interest-bearing investments or equity funds.

As You Approach Retirement

When you are no less than ten years away from retirement, you should begin investing a greater portion (more than half) of your contributions in interest-bearing investments. Strips are the investment of choice here, but be sure to choose your maturity dates carefully. You also could consider Canada Savings Bonds. A portion could simply be invested in ninety-day T-Bills and money market funds. If you have contribution room carried forward from previous years, now is the time to make those catch-up contributions that are allowed under the new RRSP rules. Since you have only a limited number of years to go until retirement, it is imperative that you have as many tax-sheltered dollars in your RRSP as possible. The only possible exception is if you have not yet paid off your mortgage, in which case you should attend to it before making further RRSP contributions.

As you approach the time when you are five years away from retiring, all your contributions should be invested in short-, medium- and long-term interest-bearing securities – T-Bills, money market funds, CSBs and strips.

From this point on, it becomes increasingly important to properly balance your investment portfolio. You have accumulated significant wealth and you are now as interested in preventing its erosion as you are ensuring its continued growth.If you have any inclination to involve yourself more heavily in financial matters, now is the time. You should be talking to your broker more often, and be more aware of financial trends – the movement of interest rates and inflation, the condition of the stock market, the health of the economy and the general mood of the investment community. Asset protection is now more important than asset growth, and an 8% or 10% virtually guaranteed return each year is, or at least should be, more attractive than a 30% return one year and the possibility of a 30% loss the next.

In the last few years before you retire, the greatest portion of your RRSP will still be in equity funds. Of course, this is a result of having bought equity funds for so many years when you were younger and the funds having multiplied in value many times. You might want to begin gradually converting these to interest-bearing investments, depending on when you plan to use them to generate retirement income. Considering the flexibility now available with RRSPs, you may not have to begin using these particular funds for another ten or fifteen or even twenty years. You would first use your other RRSP investments to generate retirement income. Thus you probably will have the option of keeping some of your equity fund investments intact for a number of years after you retire, since they will still be considered long-term investments.*

Five Strategies for Increasing the Power of Your RRSP

1. Maximizing the Return on Your RRSP Investments It is extremely important that you maximize the income on your RRSP investments. A difference of only a percentage point or two makes a huge difference in your retirement income. Earlier in this chapter we used an example where it was assumed that you made a $5,000 contribution to an RRSP at the beginning of the year which earned 10% compounded annually. After forty years, you could collect a retirement income of about $2,600 measured in today's dollars assuming an average inflation rate of 6%. This amount is taxable. If earnings in the RRSP average only 8% compounded annually, your annual retirement income expressed in today's dollars is reduced to about $1,300, which is about half the amount available if 10% is earned. If the RRSP earns 12% on average over the forty years, your annual retirement income expressed in today's dollars will be about $5,400, or more than double the amount available if 10% is earned.

2. Why Not Contribute Your Tax Refund? Many Canadians contribute to their RRSPs in February each year and then treat the tax refund they receive in April or May as found fun money. For example, if your tax rate is 35% and you contribute $2,000 to your RRSP, your tax refund will be $700 (35% of $2,000). However, if you were also to contribute the tax refund, you would greatly enhance the size of your eventual retirement income.

You could contribute the $700, but this also generates a tax

---

* When you retire, you have the option of transferring all your RRSP assets into a Registered Retirement Income Fund (RRIF). Minimum payments must be made from the RRIF each year until it is exhausted when you are ninety. This may allow you to keep a portion of your equity funds intact until you are well into your eighties. You will also have the flexibility of not being forced to sell your equity fund units when the market is depressed.

refund. Actually, if you contribute $3,080, you will generate a tax refund of $1,080 (35% of $3,080). Thus, your RRSP contribution will continue to cost you $2,000 in after-tax income ($3,080 minus $1,080), but you will have increased the size of your contribution and eventual retirement income by 54%.

3. Start Contributing Early in Your Career The earlier you begin contributing to an RRSP, the better off you will be when you retire. Assume that, in the above example, earnings on the $5,000 accumulate for only thirty years instead of forty years. Instead of generating an annual retirement income of $2,600 in today's dollars at an earnings rate of 10%, you will generate an annual retirement income of only about $1,800. Contributing the $5,000 to the RRSP ten years earlier increases your RRSP retirement income by almost 50%.

4. Contribute Early in the Year It can make a big difference in your retirement income if you contribute at the beginning of the year instead of at the end. For example, if the $5,000 contribution is made at the end of the year – twelve months later – only about $206,000 would be accumulated in the RRSP, instead of $226,000. If each year's contribution is delayed twelve months, your retirement income will be reduced by about 10%.

5. Using Spousal RRSPs You are permitted to contribute to your spouse's RRSP within your own RRSP contribution limits but deduct the amount from your own income. This allows your spouse to receive retirement income in the future that otherwise would have gone to you. You should contribute to a spousal RRSP if you know that your spouse will have less retirement income than you, and will therefore be taxed at a lower rate. This is the easiest way to split income with your spouse and should be considered by all married couples where one spouse earns considerably less than the other, and where it is likely that the higher income spouse will continue to receive most of the family income upon retiring. The lower income spouse will also eventually gain access to the $1,000 pension income deduction. Income splitting is discussed in more detail in Chapter 9.

Withdrawing Funds from an RRSP

Although RRSPs are meant to be held until retirement and to be used to fund your retirement income, you can withdraw any amount from a normal RRSP at any time. Locked-in RRSPs, which are used in special situations and from which funds can be withdrawn only in the form of a retirement income, are an exception. The amount withdrawn from the RRSP is included in income, on which tax is payable at your marginal rate. Forward averaging, a complex but effective way to reduce tax in years of high income, may help alleviate your tax liability to some extent if you withdraw funds from an RRSP.

Withdrawing funds from an RRSP is not recommended if you can possibly help it, because the economic penalty is severe. In a future year, when you have the cash available, you will not be allowed to make up for the amount withdrawn. The new seven-year carry-forward rule (for RRSP contributions not made in previous years) does not apply to withdrawals. Thus, you lose out on the tax shelter and compounding benefits. If you require extra cash, you should consider short-term borrowing to generate the necessary funds rather than collapsing your RRSP.

If it is absolutely necessary to withdraw funds from your RRSP – for instance, to buy a home or help finance your children's education or finance an emergency – you should try to withdraw the funds in a year when the tax bite will be the least severe. For example, if one spouse will be out of the work force for a year or two, he or she may escape paying tax entirely if an RRSP withdrawal is made in those years. In such a case, that spouse should be maximizing his or her RRSP contributions before the other spouse, so that such emergency cash is available with no serious tax consequences. If the other spouse's marginal tax rate is much higher than that of the spouse who temporarily drops out of the work force, a spousal RRSP should be considered. However, if spousal RRSP contributions are withdrawn within three years of their being made, they are included in the income of the spouse who originally made the contribution, and no advantage is gained.

Borrowing for Your RRSP Contribution

If you borrow to make an RRSP contribution, the interest paid on the loan is not deductible from income for tax purposes. In fact, with the seven-year carry-forward rule regarding RRSP contributions coming into effect in 1989, there is less point in incurring non-deductible debt than previously. However, if you can repay the debt relatively quickly, you should borrow to make the contribution and not count on invoking the seven-year carry-forward some years later.

Should You Realize Capital Gains or Interest in Your RRSP?

Conventional wisdom has it that you should always realize capital gains outside an RRSP and interest inside an RRSP. Since an RRSP is eventually taxed at full rates like employment or business income, you lose the benefits of realizing capital gains inside the RRSP, especially the lifetime $500,000 exemption. Interest income is taxed at full rates outside an RRSP in any case, except for that portion eligible for your $1,000 investment income deduction, so it should be earned inside the RRSP.

However, as we saw earlier in this chapter, RRSPs actually eliminate tax on your net investment. Therefore, neither capital gains nor interest is, in effect, subject to tax when earned inside an RRSP.

Nevertheless, the conventional attitude is correct if you have investments both inside and outside RRSPs. However, at this point, you are still attempting to maximize your RRSP contributions and have not yet begun a program to pay down your mortgage. Thus, all your investments are in your RRSP, so there is only one rule – maximize the return on those investments. This means investing primarily in equity funds over the long term since, historically, the stock market has outperformed interest-bearing investments. Why would you choose to earn interest at 10% when you could be earning capital gains at 15% – and neither will be subject to tax?

Only when you reach Step 6 (Chapter 9) in the formula will you consider realizing capital gains outside the RRSP and earning more interest income inside the RRSP. You will want a properly balanced investment portfolio, so there is no point in earning taxable interest outside the RRSP when it could be earned free of tax inside the plan. In fact, at some point you might consider purchasing your RRSP equity fund investments from the RRSP itself, and using cash now inside the RRSP to buy interest-bearing investments. Remember that your self-directed RRSP is like a separate person with whom (or with which) you can transact some types of business, such as buying and selling securities.

Company-Sponsored Registered Pension Plans (RPPs)

Employer-sponsored Registered Pension Plans (RPPs) are discussed in more detail in Appendix B. It is not practicable to discuss the technical aspects of these plans in great detail, because each plan is tailored to suit the particular employer/employee situation, offering a unique combination of benefits, contribution levels and membership requirements. As well, employees generally have no choice over how much they must contribute to company plans: if they are members, their annual contribution is dictated by the plan.

The pension reform introduced with the May 1985 federal budget will ensure a greater uniformity among pension plans and a much broader membership. In particular, the reform will benefit pension members' spouses, young workers and those persons who change jobs several times before retiring.

Your plan will undoubtedly undergo some changes when the pension reform proposals become law and are implemented in 1987 and succeeding years. Many changes will be minor, but a few will have a direct effect on you now and when you retire. It will be to your benefit to understand any changes that are made to your plan, particularly regarding contributions to be made by you and your employer, and any changes in eventual retirement benefits.

Will RRSPs Replace RPPs?

Some pension consultants have speculated that, with the proposed reforms, employers will be inclined to move away from defined benefit plans and instead offer money purchase plans, or even encourage employees to use RRSPs exclusively. With a defined benefit RPP, the retirement benefits are spelled out in the plan; the employer and, usually, the employee contribute sufficient amounts to the plan to provide these benefits. With a money purchase RPP, the employer and, usually, the employee contribute specific amounts each year, and the best pension possible is purchased with the accumulated funds. Money purchase RPPs are similar to RRSPs, except the employee generally has no choice as to how much he or she is required to contribute. There are at least four reasons why employers may begin to move away from defined benefit RPPs in the near future.

First, under the pension reform, defined benefit plans have become more heavily regulated, with more stringent reporting and disclosure requirements. This makes them more complicated and, therefore, more expensive to run. Money purchase RPPs, on the other hand, are much simpler to administer and much less expensive. In the extreme, RRSPs involve no employer expense except, in theory, converting the employer's previous pension contribution into additional salary for the employee.

Second, in many situations the pension benefits available under a money purchase RPP or RRSP may be better than those available under a defined benefit plan. For example, assume that you have the choice of joining (a) a defined benefit plan for fifteen years and receiving the maximum benefit available, or (b) contributing to an RRSP after having your salary adjusted appropriately. To keep the example simple, assume that your salary allows you to make the maximum $15,500 RRSP contribution each year or collect the maximum pension of $25,725 ($1,715 times 15 years – the limit in effect now).

If you do not join the pension plan, your RRSP is worth over $590,000 at the end of fifteen years, if it earns on average 11% annually. At today's annuity rates, this would provide an annual pension for life of over $60,000 a year at age sixty-five, an improvement of over $34,000. If both pensions were indexed at 6%, the difference between the two would not be as great, but would still favour the RRSP.

Third, the new pension reform rules require an employer to provide funding for at least half the pension benefit available from a defined benefit RPP. No such requirement will exist for money purchase RPPs, and one obviously does not exist for RRSPs. As well, at least one province (Ontario) apparently plans to require that benefits from defined benefit RPPs be indexed in some manner, possibly at the rate of 60% of increases in the Consumer Price Index. This will substantially increase the cost of funding defined benefit plans unless the benefits in the early years of retirement are reduced.

Fourth, in the lean and mean 1980s, many employers might prefer the certainty of funding money purchase RPPs or RRSPs according to a specific formula, as opposed to the uncertainty of defined benefit plans. With defined benefit plans, the employer must generally ensure sufficient funding is available to fund the pension contracted for in the pension agreement, no matter how much has been contributed by the employee. If earnings in the pension fund are not up to scratch or earnings rates have declined, employers must contribute additional amounts to the plan that they had not expected to contribute. With a money purchase RPP, the employer's share of the contribution is generally a specific percentage of the employee's wages, or if the employer helps the employee with RRSP contributions, a specific percentage is added to the employee's wages. Thus, if the employer knows his wage costs in advance, the pension costs are also known.

If there is indeed a trend away from defined benefit pension plans in the future, employees must be prepared to assume more responsibility for their retirement saving and investing. Those working for small- and medium-sized companies will probably be affected sooner than those in large companies where resistance to change might be stronger.

Deferred Profit-Sharing Plans (DPSPs)

Many employers sponsor Deferred Profit-Sharing Plans (DPSPs) for their employees, sometimes as an alternative to a pension plan. Under these plans, the employer makes a contribution to the DPSP each year in respect to the employee, based on a formula tied to profits made by the company and the amount of the employee's remuneration. Contributions made after 1987 immediately belong to the employee if he or she has been a member of the plan for at least two years.

DPSPs are discussed briefly in Appendix B.

Government Retirement Income

Most individuals will eventually receive retirement income from two government sources – the Canada Pension Plan (CPP) and

Old Age Security (OAS). The Canada Pension Plan operates very much like company pension plans, except that membership is compulsory for almost all Canadian workers. The contribution limits are quite low, the maximum being based on the average Canadian wage, not your particular annual earnings, and the benefits are designed to supplement private retirement benefits, not form the core of retirement income. Old Age Security is available to everyone over the age of sixty-four as long as certain Canadian residence requirements are met.

Combined maximum CPP benefits and OAS payments are intended to replace about 40% of the *average industrial wage* on retirement at age sixty-five. This should not be confused with the *average family income* on which most readers of this book will be living in the few years before retirement. The latter is considerably higher than the average industrial wage.

For example, assume that your family income is currently $45,000. Forty percent of this figure is $18,000, or $1,500 a month. Also assume that you will be eligible for maximum CPP, while your spouse will be eligible for $100 CPP a month in today's dollars. Both you and your spouse will be eligible for full OAS. This amounts to about $1,150 a month or just over 30% of your current family income. Therefore, to maintain your current standard of living, your other pension income would have to be 70% of current family income and, more importantly, would have to be indexed. Most company pension plans provide much smaller benefits than this and the benefits are not indexed.

There has been considerable concern expressed recently about whether the Canada Pension Plan will be sufficiently funded in ten or twenty years to continue paying indexed pensions. An agreement has been reached with the provinces to gradually begin raising the CPP premiums over the next two decades, but there are still some who think that the plan will become chronically underfunded. In addition, several other changes were recently made to the Canada Pension Plan, which should come into effect beginning in 1987. The most significant of these is that Canadians will be allowed to collect their CPP as early as age sixty rather than the current age of sixty-five. However, benefits will be permanently reduced by six percentage points for each year you are under the age of sixty-five, if you receive an early pension. As well, separated, divorced and widowed individuals will have much greater and fairer access to their former spouses' CPP benefits.

It is also quite likely that with tax reform, Old Age Security may shortly be available only if you meet the terms of a needs test, perhaps similar to the test that determines eligibility for the Guaranteed Income Supplement to OAS. Alternatively, much larger OAS benefits may become available only to those over the age of sixty-four who claim the refundable sales tax credit introduced in 1986, while everybody else's OAS benefits will decline or disappear.

It is probably safe to assume that benefits at about the current level will be available from the CPP when you retire. However, you should not bet the grocery money on OAS being universally available even within two or three years. Therefore, you should not plan on the government funding any more than 20% of your retirement income, unless you will be retiring on considerably less than the average wage, which is certainly not one of the goals set forth in this book.

There is little planning you can undertake to receive the maximum benefits from the CPP or OAS, since contributions to the Canada Pension Plan are mandatory. The plan allows for a drop-out period of up to 15% of your working years from the ages of eighteen to sixty-five, calculated monthly; in theory this allows for schooling beyond the age of eighteen, as well as periods of unemployment or employment outside Canada.

7

Fourth Step: Make Your Home Your Own

Periodically paying down your mortgage to the point where you can eventually pay it off will give you a great deal of financial flexibility. More importantly, it is a first-rate investment. In fact, paying down the mortgage is the same as earning tax-free income at the interest rate you are paying on the mortgage. So if you pay down $1,000 on your 12% mortgage, it is the same as earning $120 annually after tax. A risk-free investment that earns this kind of interest is not easy to find.

The Importance of Building Up Equity in Your Home

Building up equity – the difference between the value of the home and the amount you owe on your mortgage – should be at the heart of all your financial planning. It is a major, and sometimes the only, method many average Canadians have of accumulating wealth.

If an emergency arises, you can borrow against this equity by increasing the size of the mortgage. You also might borrow by means of a mortgage to provide funds for educating your children. Equity in your home improves your credit rating, which means you can borrow more easily in a conventional manner from a bank and you can borrow on more favourable terms.

And owning a home with a small or, better still, no mortgage, is one of the cornerstones of retirement planning. Shelter for the remaining years of your retirement is guaranteed. A mortgage-free home also takes the pressure off having to use limited retirement income to pay for shelter.

Finally, by building up the equity in your home, you will be able to improve the quality of your housing. When you eventually sell your first home, the cash you receive (the equity) can be used as a down payment on a larger house in a better location.

There are four ways that the equity in your home will increase. First, as you reduce the outstanding principal on your mortgage with your monthly payments, equity in your home increases. However, equity can be built up more quickly if you increase the size or frequency of your mortgage payments and/or make lump-sum payments periodically against the mortgage loan. Second, any improvements you make to your home will increase its value over time. Third, you may move to a larger house that, in absolute dollar terms, will increase in value faster than your old, smaller house. And fourth, your home will automatically increase in value over the long term – because houses always have and undoubtedly will continue to do so.

Why Paying Down the Mortgage Is a Great Investment

Almost all home-owners have, at one time or another, dwelled on the possibility of paying down their mortgage early, if only because they are disgusted with paying so much interest over such a long period of time. In the early years of paying off your mortgage, 90% or more of each payment is devoted to interest on the mortgage loan. In fact, when you are paying off only $200 or $300 principal on your mortgage in a year, it is difficult to believe that you can actually pay the whole thing off if you maintain the twenty-five-year payment schedule, and it is frightening to contemplate how much interest you will pay over that twenty-five-year period.

Unfortunately, few taxpayers actually institute a program for quickly paying down the mortgage on the family home, and even fewer understand why this is such a good investment.

I know more than one couple who have the funds available each month to pay something extra on their mortgage, but they insist on putting the dollars into Canada Savings Bonds and other safe, interest-bearing investments. Their rationale usually goes something like "the interest I'm earning is just about the same as the rate on the mortgage, so they cancel each other out."

Planning Profile

> Let's look at the case of an Ottawa couple, Marc and Moni-que Lalonde. Their interest-bearing investments return about 2% less than the interest rate on their mortgage. And to make matters worse, Marc was buying all the securities and paying tax on all the interest earned. Marc and Monique had an extra $5,000 available each year that could have been used to pay down their 12% mortgage. Instead, Marc purchased $5,000 worth of Guaranteed Investment Certificates (GICs) each year that paid 10% interest on average.
>
> Marc was already earning over $1,000 interest each year, so the interest on the GICs was fully taxable at his marginal tax rate of 35%. In the first year the Lalondes made this "investment," Marc earned $500 in interest on the GICs, but paid tax of $175, for a net return of $325. At the same time, since they did not pay down their mortgage, they "spent" an additional $600 to pay the interest expense on $5,000 of the mortgage (12% of $5,000). Therefore, because Marc was earning only $325 on the GICs after taxes, the Lalondes actually "lost" $275, which had to come out of other funds.

If Marc and Monique had used that $5,000 to pay down the mortgage, they could have saved $275 in the year. They would not have earned the interest on the GICs, but they also would not have to pay the $600 interest expense on the $5,000 portion of the mortgage. Their argument that by doing it this way, they had both the house and the investments – a sort of two-for-the-price-of-one deal – just does not hold water. To make it worthwhile buying the GICs instead of paying down the mortgage, the GICs would have had to carry an interest rate of at least 18.5%. And if mortgage rates are 12%, it is highly unlikely that any kind of security with so generous an interest rate can be found, not even high-risk bonds. Therefore, it is almost always better to use available cash to pay off a mortgage.

Even if Marc had been earning the interest on the GICs tax-free (under his $1,000 investment income deduction), they would still come out $100 short. The GICs would earn $500 (10% of $5,000) but the mortgage interest payment on $5,000 is $600.

The GICs would have to earn 12% for them to break even. Thus, paying down the 12% mortgage is exactly the same as earning a 12% rate of return, tax-free.

If you have a mortgage and also have cash available for investing, you should always compare the after-tax earnings rate on the investment you have in mind with the effective earnings rate that results from paying down your mortgage. If the mortgage interest rate is higher, pay down your mortgage. If the after-tax rate of return on the investments is higher than the mortgage interest rate – which won't happen very often – choose the investment.

If you already own interest-bearing investments, it will almost invariably be a better investment decision to cash in the securities and pay down your mortgage. Even if the securities are earning interest tax-free under your $1,000 investment income deduction, you will be better off paying down the mortgage, unless the interest rate on the securities is higher than the interest rate on your mortgage.

There is one exception to this general rule. If you are not relatively close to retirement age, you should usually choose to contribute to an RRSP (Step 3) before paying down your mortgage (Step 4). This is primarily because your RRSP will consist mostly of equity fund investments which, over the long term, should produce a higher rate of return than the interest rate on your mortgage.

By paying off the mortgage on your home, you will be providing yourself and your family with debt-free housing for the rest of your lives. In fact, a mortgage-free home will probably be the most flexible, most financially rewarding and most enjoyable asset you will ever own.

Mortgage Pay-Down Options

Almost all mortgages give you the privilege of paying off up to 10% of the mortgage principal each year on the anniversary date of the mortgage. You also can pay off any amount of the debt when you renew the mortgage.

Over the past few years, most of the financial institutions that offer mortgages have made it even easier for you to discharge your debt more quickly. Some offer completely open mortgages that allow you to pay off any amount of the principal at any time, or to renew at any time at the current interest rate. A number of mortgages permit weekly or semi-monthly payment schedules, which act to increase the amount of principal paid down annually, reduce the amount of interest paid and shorten the length of time needed to pay off the mortgage. And several institutions offer you the option of doubling up on any monthly payment of principal and interest. The extra payment is applied to reduce the principal, which means that less interest will be paid and you will pay off your mortgage sooner.

This last option provides you with a great deal of flexibility and also allows you to pay off your mortgage very quickly. For example, if you have just taken out a $70,000 mortgage at 11% amortized over twenty-five years and you choose to double up on only one monthly payment each year, you can completely pay off the mortgage in about eighteen years instead of twenty-five years. If you double up a monthly payment three times a year each year, it will take less than thirteen years to pay off the mortgage. If you double up every monthly payment, you can burn the mortgage in less than six years.

Short-Term Investing to Pay Down the Mortgage

Unless your mortgage allows you to make extra payments each month, you will generally have to wait until each annual anniversary date to pay down the mortgage. And unless you have an open mortgage, the amount you can pay down is then usually limited to 10% of the outstanding principal.

It is difficult to get an attractive return on small amounts of cash. For example, most brokers require you to invest a minimum of $5,000 in T-Bills. Generally, deposit receipts are not available in denominations of less than $5,000, and many high-interest savings accounts require as much if not more to get an attractive interest rate.

Therefore, you should investigate the money market investment funds. These invest in short-term securities such as T-Bills and generally report to you monthly. Several of these funds allow you to start investing with as little as $1,000. These funds are generally competitive with T-Bills and offer more flexibility than term deposits or high-interest savings accounts.

For smaller amounts, your only option might be a regular savings account. Shop around for the highest interest rate possible if your funds will be sitting around for longer than two or three months.

If the anniversary date of your mortgage does not fall in November, December or January, you could buy Canada Savings Bonds and cash them in at the appropriate time. They will pay a higher rate of interest than a savings account. Unfortunately, they can only be purchased at the end of October and the beginning of November.

Are Renovations Worth It?

There is a very general rule of thumb in the real estate industry: don't renovate or update your house if you expect to sell it in the near future; you probably won't get your money back on the cost of the improvements. On the other hand, if you plan to stay in your home for at least the next few years, you should get your money out of any renovations, updates, and even additions, when you eventually sell.

In theory, any improvement you make to your home should increase its value. And as your home increases in value over the years, the improvements should also share this increase. For example, if you buy a home for $100,000 and it doubles in value in eight years, it should be worth $200,000. If you put in $40,000 of improvements at the time of purchase, it should be worth $140,000 immediately after you bought it, and $280,000 in eight years (double $140,000). Thus your equity in the improved house has increased by $40,000 more than in the unimproved house.

Unfortunately, there are many exceptions to the general rule:

- In most cases, improving the lowest-priced house on the block will result in a greater percentage increase in value than improving the higher-priced homes.
- Cosmetic improvements to a home, such as painting or cleaning, almost always raise the value over the short term and can mean getting as much as $5,000 to $10,000 more on a sale. On the other hand, you may not get an

extra nickel on a sale by putting on a new roof, buying a new furnace, upgrading the electricity to 200 amps and putting in new copper plumbing. Prospective purchasers see the value of your home in terms of a variety of other factors, so the upgrades probably won't move them to consider a higher price.

- Upgrading the bathroom and the kitchen, in that order, will generally raise the value of the average older home more than knocking down walls or finishing the basement.
- Putting a $20,000 bathroom or $30,000 kitchen, or both, in an $80,000 home is probably a money-losing proposition. The cost of the renovations should be in keeping with the value of the home as a whole.
- Adding a bedroom or two, or a family room, to a home is usually cheaper than buying a larger home and will probably pay dividends in the long run. There is no sign that Canadians are moving into smaller houses, despite the fact that we are having fewer children than ever before.
- Certain types of renovations come into style periodically and go out of style as quickly. The open concept, monster bathrooms with every conceivable appliance and fixture, and the Italian kitchens that are now popular may well be out of favour in ten years. You may want to sell your home at this point and discover that your home would be worth more if you had not done the renovations.

The more quality work you can do on your home yourself, the better off you will be in the long run. Doing work that you would have paid a carpenter $3,000 to perform is just like earning $5,000, if your marginal tax rate is 40%. Normally you would have had to earn $5,000 and pay tax of $2,000 (40% of $5,000) in order to pay the carpenter.

If you are concerned about the value of your home over the short and long term, check with an established, reputable real estate agent to see whether the improvements you are contemplating will actually be of significant value. The market for homes may be such that it would be more prudent financially to move to a larger home rather than to put on an addition to your current home. Or the agent may tell you that the market is better for four-bedroom homes than three-bedroom homes, so you should scale down your plans of tripling the size of your bathroom by eliminating one of the bedrooms.

You should also pick the best, and therefore the cheapest, time of the year to have your renovations done. House contractors are generally not as busy in the winter as in the summer, and not as busy in a slack housing market as in a boom market. And when contractors are not busy, prices usually come down.

If you have a reasonable amount of equity in your home, it should be a simple matter to finance any renovations or an addition by increasing the size of the mortgage on the house.

Using Equity to Upgrade the Quality of Your Housing

The following profile illustrates how the build-up of equity can usher you into your dream home much sooner than you might have expected.

Planning Profile

Thirteen years ago, Bert and Lisa Compton bought their first home for $40,000 with $7,000 down. It was on the fringe of a trendy area in Toronto, and in six years had more than doubled in value to over $80,000 – about a 12% annual increase, two percentage points above the twenty-year Toronto average of 10%. They had made a point of optimizing location when they bought their first home and were rewarded accordingly. Over that six years, they had paid down their mortgage so that they owed only $20,000, leaving them with more than a $60,000 equity in their house after six years.

They then sold this starter home and bought a bigger home, in a better location, for $125,000 with $60,000 down and a $65,000 mortgage. (The $60,000 was what remained after taking out the costs of selling their old home.) This second home more than doubled in value over seven years to over $250,000. They had reduced their $65,000 mortgage to $50,000 over this period and now had equity of over $200,000 in their second home.

Family income had increased to the point where they felt that they could take on a larger mortgage, so a year ago they bought their dream home for $320,000, putting the $200,000 down and assuming a mortgage of $120,000. This mortgage is only about 38% of the purchase price, and is actually less onerous now, in terms of the percentage of disposable income required for mortgage payments, than the original $33,000 mortgage they had on their first home.

It took thirteen short years for Bert and Lisa to move into the home of their dreams, at least their dreams for now. Perhaps more importantly, they now have $200,000 of equity in this new home. If they had held on to their first home, which recently sold for $160,000, they would have had no more than $5,000 left on the mortgage, and therefore would have about $155,000 of equity compared to the $200,000 equity in the new home. This improvement of $45,000 resulted from their moving up to a larger home that, in dollar terms, increased in value much faster than a lower-priced home. However, the main reason why the Comptons have $200,000 equity in a home so soon (both are still in their thirties) is that they bought on a shoestring as soon as they possibly could. With their first two houses they bought location, figuring that they could put up with "imperfections" in their accommodation if they could increase their equity quickly and therefore get into their "perfect" home sooner than expected.

The Value of a Mortgage-Free Home When You Retire

How valuable is a debt-free home? Assume that you are seventy years old and you own your own home that is worth $150,000 in today's dollars. Your monthly expenses on the home are $300, including taxes, utilities and minor upkeep. You have friends living in rental accommodation that is inferior to your home in every way, but they are paying monthly rent of $950 plus $150 for utilities. You are $800 a month better off than your friends, which buys a lot of golf games and winter vacations.

You also have the flexibility that they do not. For example, assume that you tire of looking after the home, which is too big for your needs in any case, and decide to sell the house and rent an apartment. The $150,000 you get for your house could be converted into, say, a twenty-year annuity with payments that escalate at the rate of 5% each year. The payment in the initial year would be about $1,200 a month using current annuity rates, plus you would still have $300 a month available since you no longer pay taxes and utilities on the old home. Only a portion of the annuity income is taxable (you receive your $150,000 back free of tax), so perhaps you and your spouse (your spouse would be earning part of the monthly $1,200 payments resulting from the sale of the house) would pay total tax of only $200 on each payment. This leaves you with $1,000, which together with the $300 you were spending on your former home, totals $1,300. Thus, you could get rental accommodation similar to that of your friends and still have $200 left over ($1,300 minus $950 minus $150). In addition, your income from the annuity would increase each year and, with any luck, keep pace with increases in your rent for at least a few years. Your friends may not be in quite so fortunate a position.

On the other hand, you may consider buying a condominium with a portion of the proceeds from your home. Say you buy one for $100,000 and buy a similar escalating annuity with the remaining $50,000. This will produce about $330 a month after taxes during the first year of owning the condominium, which will go a long way towards paying your monthly maintenance fees and other expenses. However, you still own property that should increase in value each year. Any extra you pay in maintenance and taxes should be more than made up for with the increase in value of your condominium.

Neither of these options is as financially attractive as continuing to own the house and watching it increase in value each year. Your house should be a much better investment than either of the options mentioned above.

Should You Contribute to an RRSP or Pay Down Your Mortgage?

There are two ways to approach the question of whether you should contribute to an RRSP or use these funds to pay down your mortgage.

On purely economic grounds, you simply compare the interest rate you pay on your mortgage to the earnings rate that you expect your money to generate inside your RRSP. If the RRSP rate is higher, contribute to the RRSP.

As explained previously, paying down, say, a 12% mortgage is the same as earning a tax-free or after-tax return of 12%. And don't forget that no tax is payable on your net investment in an RRSP. The net investment is the amount that would otherwise be available to pay down your mortgage. So, you simply compare rates.

Actually, when you are younger, you should be investing the bulk of your RRSP contributions in equity funds, which over the long term should produce a return that is higher than interest rates on mortgages. Thus, in general, you would be more inclined to maximize your RRSP contributions in any particular year before you pay down your mortgage, unless you are relatively close to retiring.

In fact, when deciding whether to pay down the mortgage or contribute to an RRSP, you should be asking yourself what the tax consequences will be ten or fifteen years down the road if you begin to pay down your mortgage now instead of contributing to the RRSP. For example, say you pay off your mortgage over fifteen years and you still have twenty years to go until retirement. With a $70,000 mortgage, this could free up more than $8,000 a year for investing. You then begin an RRSP contribution program that makes up for the preceding seven years and maximizes your RRSP contribution for each current year. However, you cannot catch up on the RRSP contributions missed during the first eight years when you were paying down your mortgage. Eventually, you might begin to earn investment income that attracts tax, whereas if you had been contributing to the RRSP and were still paying off your mortgage, you would escape this future tax liability entirely, since RRSPs, in effect, eliminate tax.

The other way to approach the question is to ask yourself whether you will ever make up for the RRSP contribution if you choose to pay down your mortgage. Most home-owners will eventually own mortgage-free homes, but I suspect fewer actually would make up an RRSP contribution within the new seven-year carry-forward limit. An RRSP contribution of $1,000 earning 12% grows to over $93,000 in forty years. These are big dollars that you should not ignore. You should also bear in mind that it is more likely you will be making maximum RRSP contributions in later years, when you are earning much more income, than when you first purchase the home. At this point, paying down your mortgage with surplus funds that cannot be contributed to an RRSP because you have already made your maximum contribution makes better economic sense than trying to pay down the mortgage too early in your working career.

If you are within perhaps ten years of retiring and have not yet paid down your mortgage, you should consider eliminating this debt before making further RRSP contributions. Paying off the mortgage is like earning tax-free interest, and at this time you will be focusing more on acquiring interest-bearing investments in your RRSP. Chances are good that the interest rate on your mortgage will be higher than the interest rate on RRSP investments, so it makes sense to discharge the mortgage. You will probably still have both the time and the money to make up for the RRSP contributions using the seven-year carry-forward mechanism.

Should You at Least Develop a Small Emergency or Contingency Fund Before Beginning a Mortgage Pay-Down Program?

It is likely that investing in the type of interest-bearing securities that would make up a contingency fund will be a poorer investment than paying down your mortgage. Generally, long-term mortgage interest rates are anywhere from two to four points higher than shorter term rates that you might earn on T-Bills or Canada Savings Bonds. Of course, any interest earned would escape tax under your $1,000 investment income deduction, but paying down your mortgage is also a tax-free investment.

On the other hand, peace of mind should not be overlooked. No matter what RRSP statements may say, and despite the fact that one is living in a superb investment (your home), some Canadians insist on the security of cash being available at a moment's notice. If you are inclined this way, by all means invest a rela-

115

tively small amount in Canada Savings Bonds – say, no more than $5,000. If the bonds are paying 8% and your mortgage is costing you 11%, that is only a 3% difference on $5,000, or $150 a year, if the interest is received tax-free. Most people would consider this a small price to pay for a better night's sleep.

If you decide to invest more than $5,000 in a contingency fund, invest the next $5,000 in a money market investment fund or ninety-day T-Bills. You might earn slightly more than on the CSBs and will benefit from small hikes in interest rates. If interest rates decline, the CSBs will continue to pay the guaranteed rate until it is adjusted downward the following November. Remember that you should earn no more than $1,000 of interest annually, which can be received tax-free. If it appears that you will earn more, arrange for your spouse to begin earning some interest income from the contingency fund or, better still, start paying down your mortgage.

8
Fifth Step: Investing for Security

Comparatively few Canadians will make it to this step in the financial security formula while they are relatively young. If your family income is average and you have children, chances are that you will have little left over each year after maximizing RRSP contributions and paying down your mortgage as much as possible.

However, once you have paid off your mortgage, a significant amount of income generally becomes available. For example, payments on an $80,000 mortgage at 11% are over $9,000 a year. And if you do not have children at home – or the expenses related to them – it will probably be all that much sooner that extra income becomes available for Step 5.

In this step, investing for security can also be called "developing a contingency fund." In this sense, it is a short-term goal. However, if the funds are not used for an emergency, they become available to meet a long-term goal – supplying additional retirement income, which is addressed in the next chapter.

The emphasis is, as in previous chapters, on tax-free investing. So far, you have been maximizing your RRSP contributions (which accumulate tax-free) and paying down your mortgage (the equivalent of a tax-free investment). Some couples also may have been investing family allowance cheques in their children's names, since the children do not pay tax on any income earned. And many Canadians will have already stashed away a little of their savings as a contingency fund, for the simple reason that they sleep better at night knowing that there is a little cash they can get their hands on immediately if the need should arise.

Now is the time to take full advantage of your $1,000 investment income deduction if you are not doing so already. As was explained in Step 2, you and your spouse are each allowed to earn up to $1,000 of Canadian interest (and dividends) tax-free each year. The deduction cannot be carried forward to a following year if you do not maximize it this year.

The Nature of Contingency Funds

Traditionally, many financial planners have advised individuals to set aside an amount for emergencies as the first item in a long list of financial tactics. Usually, it is suggested that you save about three months' pre-tax income in relatively liquid investments, such as Canada Savings Bonds, and keep this amount intact indefinitely, only increasing it as your income increases or as you expect to need more for emergency spending.

As noted earlier, I disagree with this advice. Your savings can work a lot harder and more productively if they are first invested in a home and then in RRSPs. While gaining the same degree, if not better, emergency protection, your return will be greatly improved – and you will be on the road to achieving a superior level of financial security that much sooner.

The fact is that serious emergencies just do not happen very often to very many people. Of all the people you know, how many can you remember ever needing $15,000 or $20,000 on a moment's notice to fund an emergency or to tide them over for a few months because their source of income had disappeared? And if they did need this amount, how many of them had ready access to this much cash but did not have a specific emergency fund? How many were able to easily borrow this much and then had little trouble paying it back?

Also, many individuals who do manage to accumulate an emergency fund tend to spend it on non-emergencies, in which case the fund may not be there when they really need it.

Buying a home and funding your retirement rank ahead of contingency funding and additional retirement saving primarily because they offer an outstanding return on money invested; they involve little risk; they accomplish a number of objectives that improve the quality of your life; and they are flexible enough to meet a great many financial surprises during your lifetime. Owning $10,000 of Canada Savings Bonds simply does not do this as effectively – or at all in some extreme instances.

As an added bonus, what you will notice after a few years of home ownership and contributing to your RRSP is that the build-up in the value of your assets improves your credit rating tremendously – to the point where the bank begins to call you asking if you want to borrow money. This relatively quick access to a fair amount of credit at good interest rates can act as your emergency cushion until you reach Step 5. If the annual return on the leveraged investment you have in your home is in the 30% range, and you are earning 15% in your RRSP, there is no reason not to borrow at 11% or 12% and leave your home and RRSPs alone if possible.

The nature of emergency funds is to use the savings in a non-emergency situation and then rebuild the fund. For example, a number of parents, if not the majority, will use all or a portion of their emergency fund to finance their children's post-secondary education. Then, once their children finish school, they build the emergency fund up again. Many couples have used their emergency funds to buy their first home, to pay down a large portion of their mortgage, to take an extended vacation or to finance a year's sabbatical – even to help finance the purchase of their child's first home. Many others have used the emergency fund to start up a business. The truth is that not many people have emergencies that require a great amount of cash. And many average Canadians have accumulated enough assets to insulate themselves against almost any type of emergency they can think of.

For example, consider a couple who have owned their own home for ten years, making the normal mortgage payments, and have contributed $3,000 a year to their RRSPs, which earn 15% annually. They probably have a $60,000 to $100,000 equity in the home with a very manageable $30,000 to $40,000 mortgage. Their RRSPs are worth about $70,000 and they have managed to tuck away more for their children's education. In 1987, it is not unreasonable for the average couple in their mid-thirties to mid-forties to be worth in excess of $150,000, sometimes well in excess of that amount if they have done well with their home.

Their investments are not particularly liquid, but they have a great credit rating. Many could borrow $10,000 to $20,000 with just a phone call and then borrow two or three times this much in forty-eight hours, if the need should arise.

There are three lessons to be learned from this hypothetical couple:

- Do not underestimate the size and flexibility of your resources.
- Pay attention to maximizing the return on your investments.
- Do not lock yourself into an overly conservative financial corner that sacrifices long-term financial security because too much unproductive cash is on hand for situations that are likely never to arise.

How Much Should You Save in Your Contingency Fund?

How much you accumulate in your contingency fund depends on a variety of factors, most of which cannot be measured. For many people, however, an adequate amount is probably whatever both spouses can save under their respective $1,000 investment income deductions. Thus, if each of you earns an average of 8% interest on T-Bills, money market funds and Canada Savings Bonds, you will have a total of $25,000, which should see you through almost any financial emergency you care to dream up, except for the long-term unemployment of both spouses.

If you think that less than $25,000 is enough, remember that you might use money in the fund for another purpose, such as financing your children's post-secondary education. As well, the first recommendation under Step 6 in the financial security formula is to maximize your $1,000 investment income deduction if you have not already done so.

Bear in mind the comments made on income splitting previously and in Chapter 9. The point at which you reach Step 5 is also the time that you can begin to more accurately assess who is the lower income spouse and determine if that spouse will have a much lower income during your retirement years. The more disparity there is between your income and your spouse's, the more likely it is that you are needlessly paying high taxes. Tax is minimized if your incomes are identical. Each of you has your own $1,000 investment income deduction; you should ensure that each of you maximizes the benefits. As you build up your contingency fund, the lower income spouse should generally invest before the higher income spouse. This will ensure that eventually your income and your spouse's are close to the same level.

Contingency Fund Investments

Maximizing your $1,000 investment income deduction means that you and your spouse will invest in interest-bearing securities. You do not want your funds tied up in long-term investments that may be impossible to access or involve severe penalties if cashed in before maturity. Thus you will invest primarily in shorter-term, highly liquid securities.

One of the points of Step 5 in the financial security formula is to ensure that the lower income spouse has $1,000 of income eligible for the $1,000 investment income deduction during any period when he or she temporarily leaves the work force. The higher income spouse then can use the deduction to reduce his or her taxes. For this reason, the lower income spouse should be maximizing his or her $1,000 deduction before the other spouse.

At this point, both of you might already be generating a fair amount of interest income eligible for the $1,000 investment income deduction. The source of this can be cash that is waiting for the late October selling date of CSBs, cash that is waiting to be used to pay down your mortgage on the anniversary date, and cash in the bank that eventually is used for general living expenses. Thus, you should estimate how much interest you otherwise will earn each year and judge your purchase of interest-bearing investments accordingly. It would not be unusual for a person to "casually" generate $300 or $400 or $500 of interest income over the period of a year.

Invest the first $5,000 in T-Bills or a money market fund, and the second $5,000 in Canada Savings Bonds. Both are highly liquid and pay relatively attractive rates of interest. If you and your spouse want a large emergency fund, continue to split your investments among money market funds, T-Bills and CSBs until both of you have maximized your $1,000 investment income deductions. You also might consider deposit receipts, but first compare rates with T-Bills of the same maturity, as well as money market funds.

Should You Invest in Equity Funds Before Using Up Your $1,000 Investment Income Deduction?

This is an investment decision you will have to make based on your tolerance for risk. It also assumes that you have no desire to build up a contingency fund, which is perfectly acceptable if you have made it to Step 5 in the financial security formula.

However, every time that you make an investment, you should be thinking about the overall balance of your investment portfolio, as well as the quality of the investment itself. You should maximize your $1,000 investment income deduction before embarking on an equity fund purchase program to take advantage of your $500,000 capital gains exemption, simply because you are then more assured of properly balancing your portfolio. In other words, it is a conservative strategy. In addition, a significant portion of anyone's investment portfolio should be in interest-bearing investments. Why not earn this interest tax-free with your $1,000 deduction and have a liquid and flexible investment such as Canada Savings Bonds, T-Bills or a money market fund?

Otherwise, by all means take on the additional risk of investing the cash in equity funds. You will not be restricted in the type of fund you can buy and, as discussed in the next chapter, you might be able to achieve an average annual return in excess of 20%. An investment in an equity fund earning 20% annually for twenty years, ends up almost six times as large as the same amount or more invested in CSBs for twenty years at 10%. Only you can decide if the reward compensates for the increased risk over this twenty-year period.

Should You Pay Off Non-Deductible Debt Before Putting Anything in a Contingency Fund?

This question is identical to the situation outlined in the previous chapter, where Marc and Monique insisted on buying Guaranteed Investment Certificates(GICs) instead of paying down the mortgage. However, few people recognize it as being the same.

Mortgage interest is not deductible for tax purposes, nor is credit card interest, or interest paid on a loan to finance the family car. However, the rate of interest on credit cards or car loans is usually much higher than mortgage rates. In fact, some credit cards charge over 25% annual interest on overdue balances. As with mortgage interest, paying off debt with a 25% interest rate is, in effect, the same as earning interest tax-free at a rate of 25%. Paying such interest while your GICs earn interest at 10% is a foolish investment decision that, unfortunately, is made all the time. In fact, a case can be made for paying off all such high-interest debt before you invest in anything other than your home.

It is important to bear in mind that, for most people, your credit rating at your bank improves almost in direct proportion to the amount of high-interest debt you pay off. And bank borrowing rates can be 10 or 15 percentage points lower than some credit card interest rates. By paying off $1,000 of credit card interest after cashing in your $1,000 GIC, you are able to borrow at, say, 13% when and if you have to. This is certainly better than borrowing now from the issuer of the credit card at 25%.

Under no circumstances should you carry such debt and keep the GIC for liquidity in the event of an emergency. Your credit rating at the bank provides all the liquidity you need.

Balancing Your Portfolio

A balanced portfolio includes a variety of investments, each with varying degrees of risk. It will contain interest-bearing securities, as well as investments that produce dividends and capital gains. Securities may be either Canadian or foreign.

Maximizing your $1,000 investment income deduction under Step 5 in the financial security formula contributes to a balanced portfolio. By this time, you should own a home, which can be looked on as a low-risk investment. You have the bulk of your RRSP invested in equity funds which, from a conservative view-point, is considered to involve a relatively high degree of risk. However, you also have some short- and long-term interest-bearing securities in your RRSP and you are paying down, or have paid off, your mortgage. By investing in short-term interest-bearing securities under Step 5, you are adding more balance to your total portfolio.

If your portfolio is, in your judgement, perfectly balanced, the degree of risk for the portfolio taken as a whole just barely falls within the limit of your risk tolerance. This means that you are generally maximizing the return on your whole portfolio since the rate of return generally increases with the degree of risk. One person's balanced portfolio, however, might prompt another to leap out the closest window. It will take most individuals a few years to find the proper balance; but when you do, you will find that your investments are taking up almost none of your time.

In previous chapters, you have seen how specific percentages of your savings can be devoted to particular investments in order to produce a specific degree of risk. You may not be comfortable with this risk and will alter the percentage of your portfolio devoted, for example, to equity funds. Another way to increase or decrease risk is, for example, to invest in a different type of equity fund. The fluctuations in regular equity funds may not sit too well with you, so perhaps you should invest a portion of your RRSP in a balanced fund, which invests in both equities and interest-bearing securities.

You should also be concerned with striking a balance between the proportion of long-term and short-term interest-bearing securities in your portfolio. Ideally, when interest rates are high, you want to lock in a significant portion of your interest-bearing investments for the long term. When interest rates are low, you want to invest only for the short term to protect against being locked in to long-term investments that pay a lower rate of interest than that currently available.

A third factor should be kept in mind when balancing your portfolio: as your *investment horizon* decreases – that is, as less and less time remains before you want to use the invested funds – the element of risk in many investments tends to increase. This occurs primarily because you have less time to make up for poor investment choices. The superior performance of equities is valid historically only over the long term. And interest rates may not move in the direction you expect.

You are probably familiar with the general rule of thumb to use in balancing your investments: the younger you are, the more risk you can afford to accept and the more you should take. You generally have a lengthy investment horizon and therefore can weigh your total investments more heavily in favour of equities and let history take its course. When younger, you can also afford to anticipate movements in interest rates by keeping a larger percentage of your interest-bearing investments in either short-term or long-term securities. If you anticipate incorrectly, your return will be a few percentage points less for several years, but you'll probably have decades in which to make up the difference with better-performing investments.

The older you are, which generally means the closer you are to retirement, the more you should be concerned with protecting your capital. In other words, you should reduce the general level of risk in your portfolio. If you invest heavily in equities when you are five years from retirement and the market declines over the next three years, you only have two years in which to make up your losses. If you buy five-year GICs and interest rates double, your return will be much less than it could have been if you had bought short-term securities each year, and your financial security during retirement will be reduced correspondingly. In order to protect your capital, then, you should go light on equity investments and balance the maturity dates of your interest-bearing securities in such a way as to obtain a sufficiently high return to result in a level of retirement income with which you will be satisfied.

Remember that the optimum balance of your portfolio will change over the years. You will not reach a point overnight where all new investments should be in conservative, interest-bearing securities. You should review your portfolio once every year to ensure that your overall return is attractive and that the balance of investments is still within your risk tolerance level and meets your expectations for the movement of interest rates.

Average Canadians will have most of their portfolio investments in an RRSP until they are relatively close to retirement age. At various times, you will also have some money invested outside RRSPs to take advantage of the $1,000 investment income deduction. As you approach retirement age, you may have more invested outside the RRSP to take advantage of the $500,000 capital gains exemption (as described in the following chapter). Some taxpayers will also have funds invested in the names of their children to provide for their education (Step 7). In addition, your home is an investment that increases in value over the years, particularly if you pay down the mortgage.

Figure 8.1: The Traditional Security Pyramid

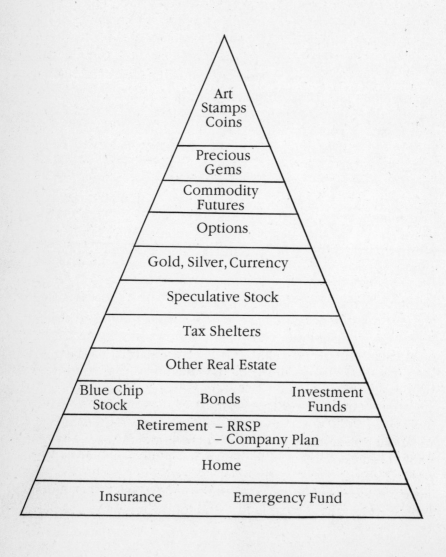

The Security Pyramid

How much should you put into the various investments? It depends on you and your personal situation, as well as your tolerance to risk. There are no hard and fast rules. One common approach, however, is to use the security pyramid, a representation of which can be seen in Figure 8.1.

In theory, you begin building at the bottom of the pyramid by first putting something away for emergencies and by buying insurance. Moving to the next level, you buy a home and then move up to begin saving for your retirement (using conservative investments). Only when you have taken care of these financial necessities do you begin taking more risks with your investments. Continuing up the pyramid, we find blue chip shares, government bonds and investment funds. Of more risk are some real estate investments, some types of tax shelters and more speculative stocks. Then the pyramid moves into precious metals, currency speculation, options, commodities and finally precious gems, coins and art. The items at the top have the potential for huge appreciation but can also prove to be almost worthless overnight. They are extremely high-risk investments and should be left to gamblers and experts. Most of the investments in the pyramid are much too speculative, and almost all require too much time and expertise to be considered by the average Canadian. Hence, only eight investments have been recommended.

The Simplified Security Pyramid The pyramid concept is quite valid, so I have presented my own interpretation below. Of course, the pyramid reflects the seven steps in the financial security formula.

As in the traditional pyramid, life insurance is still at the foundation. The next two items – home and retirement saving (primarily RRSP) – take up much of the room in the structure. Home is listed first because it should be purchased before you begin contributing to your RRSP for retirement, although eventually retirement savings might form a larger portion of your total wealth. Higher up on the pyramid, you institute a mortgage paydown program, you invest to take advantage of tax-free income using your $1,000 Canadian investment income deduction and your $500,000 capital gains exemption, and you shift interest

Figure 8.2: The Simplified Security Pyramid

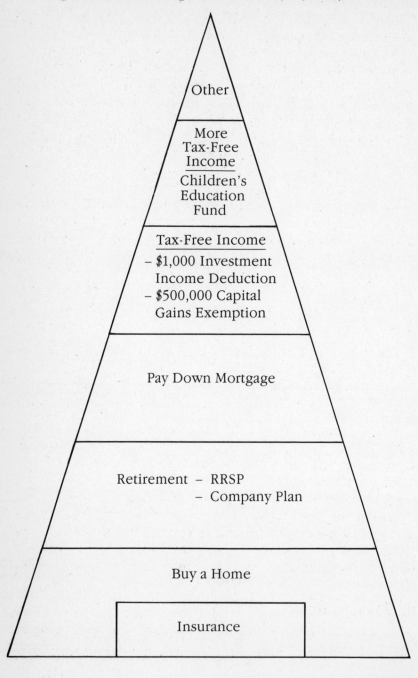

Other

More
Tax-Free
Income

Children's
Education
Fund

Tax-Free Income

– $1,000 Investment
Income Deduction
– $500,000 Capital
Gains Exemption

Pay Down Mortgage

Retirement – RRSP
– Company Plan

Buy a Home

Insurance

income to your children where it will escape taxes. Finally, at the top of the pyramid, you leave the financial security formula behind since you have achieved all your objectives, and if you so desire, begin to invest more speculatively.

In the standard pyramid, insurance and saving for emergencies always appear at the bottom. I agree with this placement of insurance although its importance should not be overstated. But there is no point in putting away $20,000 earning 10% of perhaps non-taxable interest for an emergency, when you could use that cash for a down payment on a home and watch it "earn" 25% or 30% a year as your house appreciates in value.

And the surest, safest and least worrisome route to financial security for the average Canadian is to have a fully paid-off home and to maximize tax-sheltered retirement savings (RRSPs) and company pension plans. Hence these two items assume the greatest importance in the simplified pyramid.

It might appear that a great deal of emphasis has been placed on investing in equity investment funds relative to the other seven investments recommended in this book. Bear in mind, however, that equity funds are a long-term investment – requiring at least ten years to fulfill their maximum return potential. Thus you might have 80% or 90% of your portfolio in equity funds in your RRSP, when you are in, say, your mid-thirties. But when you take into account both the equity in your home and your mortgage pay-down program, this percentage, relative to your *total* investments, could easily shrink below 50%. And this is perfectly acceptable for someone with twenty-five to thirty years to go before retirement. Remember that the paying down of your mortgage, for example, is also considered to be the equivalent of owning tax-exempt interest-bearing securities. As you get closer to retirement, the makeup of your portfolio will not change appreciably. Although more and more of your new investing will be directed towards lower-risk interest-bearing investments, amounts previously invested in equity funds will continue to grow in value.

Three Sample Portfolios

No one can tell you exactly how to balance your portfolio. The division among the various investments depends on your current financial situation, your age and tolerance for risk. However, the following sample portfolios, designed for three different types of situations, may help you get a rough idea of what balance is most appropriate for you.

There are four essential elements in these balanced portfolios:

1. Some risk – equity funds;
2. Little risk – long-term interest-bearing securities, such as strip bonds, income funds, GICs;
3. Very little risk – short-term interest-bearing securities, such as Canada Savings Bonds, T-Bills, money market funds and deposit receipts; and
4. No risk – mortgage pay-down program plus equity in your home.

Portfolio 1: Younger couple with young children and a home; lower income spouse has just re-entered work force.

  30% – equity funds
   5% – short-term interest-bearing securities
  65% – home, primarily equity built-up

This couple has a small pool of short-term cash, some in a savings account and the rest invested in a money market fund in their RRSPs. Almost all new investment is in RRSP-eligible equity funds followed by their mortgage pay-down program.

Portfolio 2: Couple in their late thirties or in their forties with teen-age children and a home; both spouses have been working for a number of years.

  40% – equity funds
   5% – long-term interest-bearing securities
  10% – short-term interest-bearing securities
  45% – home, equity and mortgage pay-down

This couple's new investment would first go towards RRSP-eligible equity funds and then to paying down the mortgage. Once the mortgage is paid down, they should consider additional long- and short-term interest-bearing investments while continuing to invest in equity funds, bearing in mind they may have to fund a portion of their children's college education.

Portfolio 3: Empty nest couple, five years prior to retirement.

30% – equity funds, shifting from inside to outside RRSP
25% – long-term interest-bearing securities, primarily in RRSP
10% – short-term interest-bearing securities
35% – home, all equity

All new investment has for the past few years gone into interest-bearing investments and will continue to do so, primarily in their RRSPs. Equity investments in their RRSPs are gradually being sold and replaced with long-term interest-bearing securities. Investments outside their RRSPs are made first in interest-bearing securities to take advantage of the $1,000 investment income deduction, then in equity funds to take advantage of the $500,000 capital gains exemption. The percentage of funds invested in short-term and long-term interest-bearing securities could change over the years, depending on market conditions.

Investing in a Volatile Economic Environment

Nobody is equipped to tell you exactly when to move in and out of certain investments, not even the experts. But there are a few general rules. If inflation and interest rates are on the rise, you should be in short-term securities; when rates peak you should lock in the high rate for the long term. If the economy moves into anything resembling a recession, you should go light on your equity positions and load up when the economy shows signs of recovery. The old adage "Buy low and sell high" will always produce wealth; unfortunately, no one ever predicts with any accuracy when the highs and lows will occur. So if you miss investment cycles, you most certainly will not be alone.

There are two approaches to take, however, that will ensure you do at least as well as the next person. The first is to listen to and invest with the experts. Pay attention to longer-term trends, specifically changes in interest and inflation rates, as well as the general trend of the stock market and the health of the economy. Listen to your broker and use investment funds when possible because, even though they participate in all phases of the investment cycle, the effects of downturns can be minimized if the management is good, and they can make hay on the upturns.

Also, stick to shorter-term interest-bearing investments, unless you are satisfied with current "high" interest rates and the consensus among experts is that interest rates have peaked and should begin dropping in the near future.

The other approach is to ignore market conditions and *dollar average* your investments instead. This is just another way of describing the process whereby you invest a specific amount each month (or quarter, or year) and stick to your plan no matter what. You might invest in an equity fund when the market is high and due for a drop, but you will also invest when it is unusually low and poised to surge to new highs. Thus, you will be assured of at least an average return based on long-term trends – and the long-term trend in the stock market has been up. This method has the added advantage of reducing risk, in that you are relying exclusively on long-term averages and not on your, or someone else's, ability to always anticipate the correct movement of short-term fluctuations in the financial marketplace.

The same dollar-averaging method also applies to purchases of long-term interest-bearing securities – although, unfortunately, it is not as foolproof, particularly if you invest in exceptionally long-term securities such as twenty-year strips. For example, you might invest at 10% or 12% over several years, which looks relatively attractive. However, there is no guarantee that the fundamentals of the economy will not change so that the norm for inflation becomes 12% and interest rates never go below 16% or 17% while you are stuck with 10% securities that do not mature for another fifteen years. You should only lock in long-term yields if you feel that interest rates are high and will likely remain stable or decline over the next few years, or if you are satisfied with the return and do not want to think about your investment again for twenty years. Taking the latter approach, however, generally does not lead to a significant level of financial security. You should also bear in mind that you can probably sell your long-term strips, perhaps at a loss, and wait for interest rates to go up even further before you again commit yourself to a long-term investment in a strip.

Caring For Your Investments

Generally speaking, the less attention you pay to the financial world, and the less you are aware of movements in interest rates, the stock market and the economy in general, the happier you will be with your investments. If you read the financial pages every day, you will always, and I mean every single day, find that there are plenty of investments performing better than yours – sometimes fantastically better. However, most of these investments also involve a great amount of risk and possibly require specialized knowledge, as well as huge amounts of capital to invest. If you had invested in any of them, you might soon be catatonic from worry.

This is not to say that you should cultivate a total ignorance of financial matters. Your investments will do better on average over the long term if you are aware of the general health of the economy, simply because you will get out of unproductive investments sooner and into higher-return investments earlier than you might otherwise.

Once you reach Steps 5 or 6, you should consider using a broker. His or her advice will be invaluable, and the overall return on your investments is more likely to improve. You may even want to begin using a broker once you have a few thousand contributed to your RRSP. At the earliest opportunity, you should also try to develop a balanced investment portfolio that initially, at least, is heavily weighted towards interest-bearing securities that provide a good, secure return. Try to be satisfied with attractive, secure returns, even though they may not be the best at that particular time. Remember the old tax-planning adage: "Pigs get fat, hogs get slaughtered." Remember, too, that you are investing mostly for the long term. Finally, set dollar goals for your shorter-term investments, and be satisfied when you achieve them.

Using the Experts

One of the primary objectives of this book is to minimize the worry and effort required to achieve above-average financial security. One sure way of staying on the path to this goal is to let the financial experts do as much of your decision making as possible.

Realistically, the average Canadian who holds down a full-time job can't hope to become a financial expert, let alone financially sophisticated. Even if you have some background and a burning interest in the field of investment, you simply do not have the time available to become reasonably knowledgeable about even a small section of the financial marketplace. There are thousands of people in the financial centres of Canada, and hundreds of thousands worldwide who spend practically every waking hour concentrating all their energies on tiny facets of the financial arena. Of these, there are only a handful of acknowledged investment experts, and almost all of these people have bad years once in a while. Financial wizards are like movie stars – precious few have any staying power and they all bomb at the box office periodically. Any average Canadian who thinks he or she can invest like the experts and get the same kind of returns runs the considerable risk of bombing almost non-stop.

In any case, why would you want to spend the time so fruitlessly when the odds are stacked so heavily against success. The experts are more than willing to do your decision making for you – for a fee of course. All you have to do is choose your experts reasonably carefully, sit back and let history take its course as far as investment returns are concerned.

Most people have easy access to four primary sources of financial and investment expertise: financial literature, their banker, their broker, and the professional managers of investment funds.
Financial Literature A wealth of financial information is available to you in most daily newspapers, as well as in any magazine rack or bookstore. It is also available, usually free, from financial institutions, investment dealers and brokers, stock exchanges, insurance companies, financial associations, accountants, lawyers and myriad financial consultants and counsellors. Unfortunately, the huge amount of material available can be very confusing for the uninitiated and almost all of it is written for the financially sophisticated. Most of it will be of only limited use to you, except:

- Tax return preparation manuals, the best being
  Preparing Your Income Tax Returns, published
  annually by CCH and written by R.D. Hogg and M.G.
  Mallin of the accounting firm Arthur Anderson. It

provides all the tax information you are likely to need – although, unfortunately, in a relatively technical manner.

- Any guide that provides detailed information on budgeting, and then only if you are having a problem putting enough aside to achieve your financial goals. Free booklets are available from several of the major banks and trust companies, as well as several insurance companies.

- The financial pages of your newspaper, or business publications such as *The Financial Post* or *Financial Times*, can be useful to keep abreast of inflation and interest rate trends, stock market movements and the general health of the economy. Unfortunately, there is no guarantee that you or anyone else will read the signs correctly.

Your Banker Your banker can also be the manager of a trust company, a credit union, a savings and loan corporation or a *caisse populaire*. While usually not investment experts, they are almost always very good, conservative money managers who can steer you clear of dubious investments and inform you of the advantages of others. The more you deal with a particular bank, the more helpful it will become. The bank makes money from handling your finances – both from lending the money you have on deposit in various forms and lending you other people's money. Take advantage of your banker's expertise and do not hesitate to demand what you consider to be the best service. You are the customer whether you are depositing money or borrowing it, and the bank is the seller. You always have the option of taking your business elsewhere if you don't like the service you get.

Your banker can sell you several of the eight investments, recommended in this book, including savings accounts, deposit receipts, GICs and Canada Savings Bonds. As well, he or she might be able to act as your agent in the purchase of strips, T-Bills and even investment funds. You can open an RRSP with your banker and he or she might also offer self-directed RRSPs. You should shop around, however, to ensure that you pay the minimum annual administration fee.

Stockbroker As the size of your investment portfolio increases and the complexity of your investments expands, you will probably find it necessary to use a stockbroker. Investment dealers and brokers do much more than simply buy and sell stocks for you. Many are now in direct competition with your bank. Of the eight recommended investments, it might be more convenient to use a broker to purchase strips, T-Bills and investment funds.

The job of a broker is to offer investment advice and hope that his or her clients follow that advice and make lots of money, thereby earning the broker lots of commissions. This brings to light one of the drawbacks of dealing with some brokers. They make their money only when executing financial transactions on your behalf. The more transactions carried out, the more money they make. A broker will generally allocate his or her time based on the potential your portfolio has for generating commissions. However, better brokers take the long-term point of view: they recognize that it's more worthwhile to forego large commissions today, and have you as a client for the twenty years it might take for the value of your portfolio to reach six figures. Shop around until you find one to your liking.

A broker can be much more valuable than you may at first think. First, cash on deposit with a broker generally earns daily interest at a rate that is at least competitive with a bank's, if not slightly better. You can purchase all the recommended investments through a broker, including units in any investment fund. In fact, the front-end load, or commission charged by some investment funds, may be reduced if units are purchased through a broker. Finally, brokers offer self-administered RRSPs.

Once you have accumulated a reasonably large portfolio, it is recommended that you find and use a broker. Most won't mind if you are not trading regularly, as long as you do not take up too much of their time. Also, unless you know exactly what you are doing, you should generally steer clear of discount brokers, despite the attractiveness of their lower commissions. Part of a broker's job is to warn you against doing stupid things, or at least suggesting that you sit back and think your decision over for a day or two. Discount brokers simply carry out your orders and offer no advice. However, if you have decided to buy into an investment fund that carries a front-end load, you may find that load charges are substantially reduced if you place your order through a discount broker.

Experts through the Investment Funds The assets of every investment fund are managed by one or more professionals who use their expertise to spot the best growth opportunity for the fund. If the managers do well, the fund does well, so be sure to study the track record of a fund before you buy. If a fund's management is no longer performing well – as sometimes happens if there is a personnel change – you simply sell your units and buy into a fund that shows a better growth potential.

Of course, these professional managers charge a fee for their expertise. Many funds charge a front-end load when you buy, ranging up to 9% of the purchase price, and all charge an annual administration fee ranging up to 2% of the value of the units you buy.

The front-end load should discourage you from switching funds very often. In any case, however, you really should be looking at long-term performance of a few funds, not the short-term, month-to-month performance of a variety of funds. The *Financial Times* and *The Financial Post* publish a monthly performance guide to almost all the Canadian funds. When choosing funds, you should study these guides closely to narrow your choice of funds down to a manageable few. Then you may want to talk to your broker about which funds he or she would recommend.

The Benefits of Filling Out Your Own Tax Return

It took me by surprise fifteen years ago to learn that perhaps as many as two-thirds of Canadians have someone else they think is competent prepare their tax returns. That fraction probably has not changed, despite the new, simplified tax form. (An even "simpler" tax form is apparently being designed at this writing.) In addition, there are many instruction books now available on filling out your own form, and Canadians, in general, are better informed about taxes today than they were fifteen years ago. Yes, the tax rules are much more complex now, but not for the average person whose primary source of income is employment and who has no more than half a dozen deductions.

Every Canadian should at least make one attempt to fill out his or her own tax return. It could become a habit. But even if you get bogged down and have to get "professional" help, at least you will have learned something of the tax system, which in the long run may make you appreciate more keenly the necessity of setting financial goals and following a well-defined path towards financial security. There are also other advantages to struggling with your own tax return:

Are You Missing Out on Legitimate Deductions? If you make it through to the bitter end, you may discover whether or not you have been missing any deductions in past years that could lower your tax bill. A few years ago, one of the typists in the firm where I worked asked if she could claim a larger deduction for her mother. The typist and her sister wholly supported their mother who had been resident in Canada for only two years and had no income. The typist had been reading her tax return and dis-covered that she might be eligible for the "equivalent to mar-ried" deduction rather than the ordinary deduction available for dependent parents. Indeed she was, and her tax refund that year was $400 larger than she expected.

Many Canadians pay too much tax for no other reason than ignorance of very simple pieces of tax law. Going through your tax return line by line, carefully reading the accompanying Reve-nue Canada guide, as well as using one of the tax return prepara-tion guides (available in bookstores during February, March and April), are the easiest ways you have of paying less tax and therefore increasing the funds you have available. They will also help an outside preparer lower your tax bill. He or she cannot deduct an item from income if you don't tell them about it, and few of the "budget-priced" preparers spend enough time with you to discover all the deductions to which you may be entitled.

The computer programmers' maxim – "garbage in, garbage out" – is appropriate. If you insist on having someone else prepare your return, look on this person as a professional who is being paid to dot your i's and cross your t's, and to confirm your calculations after you have struggled with your return for a few hours. You will pay less – both for your tax bill and in fees for the preparation. One more thing. Consider going to someone who has spent the past few years in the tax field, not someone who spent the past weekend being "trained" in the preparation of tax returns. "Garbage out" also applies to the preparation side of the tax return business.

The Joy of Non-Taxable Income! Filling out your own return can impart a fine appreciation of the difference between taxable and non-taxable income. Seeing the federal and provincial governments take 30% or 40% of the income you earned from January to December hurts, particularly if you have to write a cheque for taxes owing. But deducting the $1,000 of Canada Savings Bond interest you earned over the year or the $5,000 RRSP contribution you made should bring home the importance of investing effectively if you want to achieve a superior level of financial security.

9

Sixth Step: Investing for Gain

The accumulation of wealth under Step 6 is what will make you exceptionally comfortable later in life. It's the icing on the cake. You will have paid off the mortgage on your home and will be eligible for a good pension from your company plan and/or your RRSPs – an excellent pension if you have been maximizing your RRSP contributions for twenty or thirty or forty years. Nevertheless, it is this additional retirement income that will finance that once-in-a-lifetime, around-the-world cruise, or that winter condo in Florida. Of course, you also might use the savings under Step 6 to finance a portion of your children's education or a year-long sabbatical, or an extended vacation, or even for an emergency.

In a sense, the extra income that becomes available once you reach Step 6 is really spare cash – at least, spare cash in the context of achieving the four financial goals. Consequently, you can afford to take on some increased risk as you invest these funds, even if you are within five or ten years of retiring. In fact, since you have been maximizing your RRSP contributions and you have paid off your mortgage, you can view this additional retirement saving as relatively long term. Your basic retirement income needs have been – or will be – satisfied, so this funding may not be required until many years after you have retired.

First, if you have not already done so, maximize your $1,000 investment income deduction. Many couples will be happy with a relatively small contingency fund and may only be earning perhaps $1,000 of interest between them. You have invested in sufficient short-term securities, so now the remaining interest eligible for the deduction could come from longer-term Guaranteed Investment Certificates (GICs). Remember, however, that your GICs will be more or less inaccessible until the maturity date, unless you are willing to pay a relatively hefty penalty to dispose of them.

You also might consider a mortgage or bond income investment fund. Both are relatively liquid investments, but the value of your bond fund units will generally fluctuate more widely with swings in interest rates than will a mortgage fund. If interest rates are rising rapidly, the bond fund may actually lose value during the year, despite receiving interest on its investments that is eligible for your $1,000 deduction. Thus, bond funds should be looked upon as long-term investments.

Once you have maximized your $1,000 deduction, it is time to take maximum advantage of the $500,000 capital gains exemption. You can do this by investing in equity funds – as long as you plan to hold them for at least five years and preferably more than ten years. If you plan to use these funds relatively soon, perhaps to take an extended vacation or to augment your retirement income, you should focus on more conservative equity funds that stress dividend income.

Once you have paid off your mortgage and taken care of funding your children's education, it would not be unusual for up to $10,000 a year or more to become available, after maximizing your RRSP contributions. If you have much more than this, the excess would be considered discretionary income, and you might think about obtaining professional advice to help you with your investment planning.

Maximizing Your $500,000 Lifetime Capital Gains Exemption

Beginning in 1985, the first $500,000 of capital gains realized by individuals resident in Canada is exempt from tax. This covers the one-half of a capital gain that is normally included in income for tax purposes, which in effect means that the tax rate on capital gains is half the rate on normal income before taking into consideration the $500,000 exemption. The actual limit for the exemption is phased in over six years. The accumulated maximum that can be claimed is as follows:

Year	Capital Gain	Taxable Portion of Capital Gain Exempt from Tax
1985	$20,000	$10,000
1986	$50,000	$25,000
1987	$100,000	$50,000
1988	$200,000	$100,000
1989	$300,000	$150,000
1990	$500,000	$250,000

All capital gains must be reported in your tax return and the exempt portion is then claimed on form T657, which is available from your district taxation office.

Gains from all sources, including the sale of non-arm's-length capital assets such as family businesses, the sale of foreign capital assets and the sale of a vacation property are eligible. Any gain you realize when you sell your principal home remains tax-exempt under a different set of rules, and such a gain does not reduce the amount of other gains eligible for the $500,000 exemption.

A number of changes have been made with the introduction of the $500,000 capital gains exemption, including the following:

- Capital gains are no longer eligible for your $1,000 investment income deduction.
- Cash bonus payments received from Canada Savings Bonds are now considered to be interest and not capital gains, but only one-half of the bonus is taxable.
- Capital gains that are realized under an employee stock option plan and that accrue to the time the option is exercised do not qualify for the $500,000 exemption.
- Individuals are no longer able to deduct up to $2,000 of allowable capital losses – that is, one-half of the full capital loss of $4,000 – from all sources of income. Capital losses now simply reduce capital gains realized in the year or are applied to effectively increase the size of your $500,000 exemption.
- Most stock dividends no longer receive capital gains treatment and are treated like regular cash dividends.

- A variety of other changes specifically affect farmers, owners of small business corporations, persons emigrating from Canada, etc. Some of these changes may be explained in your tax return; otherwise, information is available from your local district taxation office.

The exemption was initially criticized for offering a benefit only to the rich, whose wealth consists primarily of capital assets. However, there is no reason why the average wage earner cannot also benefit if he or she has accumulated savings and has acquired a relatively balanced investment portfolio. Many equity investment funds produce primarily capital gains that are eligible for the $500,000 lifetime exemption. As well, capital gains or losses may be realized with income investment funds, as well as on strips, T-Bills and GICs if they are sold prior to maturity.

A number of commentators have suggested that the capital gains exemption may be short-lived. And even if it survives tax reform over the next few years, as well as the government's need for additional revenue, it may be altered radically enough in the future that its benefits will be watered down. Therefore, if you currently own capital property – such as stock in public or private companies, other types of capital securities, and other types of property (for example, a vacation home, jewellery, works of art or antiques) – you might want to preserve the tax-exempt status of any accrued gain by selling the property.

If you don't wish to dispose of the particular property, one easy solution is to sell it to your spouse at fair market value. Keep in mind, however, that if you do not receive reasonable consideration from your spouse, which could take the form of a note payable as well as cash, the attribution rules will apply to future income and capital gains earned on the property. This may or may not be of concern, depending on how long you intend to hold the property. If no fair market value can be readily established, you should have the property professionally appraised to support the sale price in case you are challenged by the tax authorities. You must elect in your return to transfer property to your spouse at fair market value. A simple letter of intent will usually suffice.

You also might consider selling the property to your children, perhaps by means of a trust so that you retain control of the property throughout your lifetime. Such sales or transfers to anybody other than your spouse automatically occur at fair market value for tax purposes.

Additional Retirement Saving – Investments

If you expect that it will be at least ten years before you want to use additional retirement savings, your major investment focus should be on equity funds that generate primarily capital gains. The lower income spouse should invest before the higher income spouse.

Since you are not investing inside your RRSP, you will have a much wider range of funds to choose from, including funds that invest in U.S., Japanese and other foreign securities. Several of these funds have exceptional earnings records, and some of the international funds may, assuming good management, have a better chance of weathering temporary market downturns. This is because their investments will be spread over a number of countries whose markets on average may be more healthy than the Canadian stock market.

At least half a dozen non-RRSP equity funds have averaged returns of better than 20% compounded annually over the past ten years, which is considerably better than funds that are eligible for RRSPs. A return of this magnitude can produce spectacular results. For example, if you contribute only $500 a year for twenty years to a fund that earns 20%, you will accumulate over $110,000. If inflation averages 6%, this is about $35,000 in today's dollars.

At this stage, you should consider investing all your additional retirement savings income in the best performing funds available. Do your research carefully on the funds you buy. It is unlikely one fund will continue to earn, say, 25% compounded annually, whereas it is more likely that three different funds, on average, will be able to earn at least 20% if they have good track records.

Once you have reached Step 6, it becomes more difficult to say exactly how much you should invest in equity funds. It is now becoming extremely important that you balance your portfolio to suit future needs. Most Canadians who reach this stage in the formula will no longer be in their twenties or thirties, which means always keeping one eye on your retirement needs when you make any investment. However, it will generally be safe to invest in these equity funds almost indefinitely, as long as you are balancing your portfolio by acquiring interest-bearing investments in your RRSP.

If you feel that your additional retirement savings fund will not survive the ten-year horizon, you should consider investing in more conservative equity funds that stress dividends and do not fluctuate in value as much as those that stress capital gains. You will be taxed more lightly on dividend income than on interest income and should still realize capital gains. If you happen to need the funds during a temporary downturn in the market, you can always use your contingency fund money and keep the equity fund investments intact until the market recovers.

You may want to consider an equity fund savings plan. For example, you might contribute, say, $100 a month to each of three different funds. You would make the contributions no matter what the state of the stock market – high or low or undecided. In this way, you do not miss contributing when the market is depressed, even though you may make some contributions at market peaks that subsequently decline in value. Remember that you are investing for the long term, and over the long term the stock market has outperformed interest rates.

Lowering the Family Tax Rate by Splitting Income with Your Spouse

Income splitting with a spouse is usually defined as the process of having income, which would normally be taxed in the hands of the higher income spouse, earned by and taxed in the hands of the lower income spouse so that less tax or no tax is paid on that income. It can also be defined more generally as ensuring that there is as little difference as possible between the taxable incomes of each spouse. Like the $500,000 lifetime capital gains exemption, income splitting has been viewed as the preserve of the rich. However, average Canadians can play too, and reap significant benefits.

The Attribution Rules

You should be aware that the Income Tax Act contains certain regulations, called *attribution rules*, that discourage income splitting. Under these rules, all investment income – including interest, dividends and capital gains – earned on funds transferred by you in any manner to your spouse is taxed in your hands and not in your spouse's hands, even though that income now legally belongs to your spouse. A transfer includes a gift, a loan or a sale, whether made directly, or indirectly, through a trust or another third party. Considered to be a loan are guarantees made by one spouse on a third-party loan to the other spouse, as well as third-party loans where one spouse pays the other's interest expense.

There are six specific situations in which the attribution rules do not apply, even though there has been a transfer from one spouse to the other:

1. Spousal Loans If interest is paid on the loan by the recipient of the funds (that is, the lower income spouse) from his or her own funds, the attribution rules do not apply. The funds used to pay the interest include income earned by the spouse as a result of investing the loaned funds. The interest must be paid each year, or within thirty days of the year end, and the loan must bear interest at a rate no lower than the commercial rate in effect at the time the loan was made or the prescribed rate at that time. (The *prescribed rate* is the interest rate that the government charges on late tax payments or pays after April 30 on taxes that are refunded.)

2. A Sale to Your Spouse of Assets Owned by You The attribution rules do not apply if the sale is made at fair market value, and if you receive consideration from your spouse equal to the fair market value of the asset. Such consideration must have originally belonged to your spouse – in other words, you cannot give your spouse cash to pay for the asset – or the consideration may consist of debt, such as a note payable by your spouse. Such a note must bear interest on the same terms as those for a spousal loan, and your spouse must pay the interest each year, or within thirty days of the year end, with funds that belong to the spouse.

3. A Transfer that Results in Your Spouse Earning Business Income In this case you may give or lend your spouse funds in any manner whatever, without coming under the attribution rules.

4. A Salary Paid to Your Spouse Attribution rules do not apply, so long as the salary is paid for work performed in a business owned by you, and so long as it is reasonable in relation to the duties performed by your spouse.

5. Any Transfer of Funds or Assets that Is Ordered by a Court as a Consequence of the Permanent Breakdown of the Marriage Essentially, the attribution rules cease to apply after the marriage breakdown.

6. Upon the Death of Either Spouse or at the Point the Spouse Who Transfers the Asset Becomes a Non-Resident of Canada In either situation, you should seek professional guidance to ensure any taxes are minimized.

Equally important to many Canadians, the attribution rules do not apply to couples who live together but who are not legally married, whether or not they may be considered married under their relevant provincial family law. In this situation, the higher income partner can give or lend funds to the lower income partner, and any income earned will be taxed in the lower income person's hands. This is one of the reasons why there is not a great deal of incentive to get married in this country – at least from the point of view of keeping taxes to a minimum.

How Significant Are the Savings?

Assume, for example, that:

- You would normally earn $50,000 in 1987;
- Your spouse has temporarily left the work force and has no source of income;
- Somehow you manage to arrange things so that each of you now earns $25,000 for tax purposes (the attribution rules will make this difficult, however); and
- 1987 tax rates are used, where the provincial rate of tax is assumed to be 50% of federal tax payable, and only personal exemptions are taken.

Without income splitting in 1987 (where you earn $50,000 and your spouse earns nothing), your tax bill would be about $14,300.

However, with the total family income split in half, each of you now pays tax of about $5,800 for a total of about $11,600. This results in a saving of about $2,700 ($14,300 minus $11,600). Very few couples will be able to split their income in half like this to maximize savings in their working years, but most can arrange to have the lower income spouse earn more income than he or she normally would in every year of the marriage. If an income-splitting program is started now, you will begin to experience the tax savings much sooner, and it is much more likely that you and your spouse will be able to achieve a fifty-fifty split of income by the time you both retire.

Six Techniques for Increasing the Income-Earning Potential of Your Spouse

Over the past few decades it has become easier to arrange effective income-splitting programs because in many cases both spouses have lengthy income-earning careers. Only rarely does one spouse permanently stop earning income the moment he or she gets married. However, even though both spouses may be earning work-related income (as opposed to investment income), it is not uncommon for one spouse to earn considerably more than the other each year and to earn more in total over the couple's working lifetime. Thus, to more easily explain the following income-splitting ideas, it is assumed that there is a lower income spouse who will always earn less than the other member of the partnership, and who will always have a lower marginal rate of tax.

The first three of the six income-splitting techniques outlined below should be considered by couples of all ages, particularly younger couples. The next two techniques will be of interest only to couples who have reached Step 6 in the financial security formula. The last technique applies only to those couples where one or both spouses are self-employed and own a business.

1. Who Pays for Family Expenses? Rather than splitting family expenses and investment earnings at all times during any marriage, the higher income spouse should always pay for all family expenses, while the lower income spouse should channel all his or her income into investments. The lower income spouse's income will thus be continually augmented by this extra investment income that otherwise would have been earned by the higher income spouse. This investment income will be taxed at a lower rate in the lower income spouse's hands, thus reducing the total family tax bill, which allows more funds to be devoted to achieving the four financial objectives. There is no legal onus on a married couple to split household and other expenses evenly, and you will not be attacked under the attribution rules if one spouse uses all his or her income for investment purposes.

In the same vein, the higher income spouse should pay the lower income spouse's taxes, if possible, thus freeing up more of the lower income spouse's earnings for investment purposes. One Montreal couple do this regularly. She is a freelance writer with an annual tax bill that has averaged $4,000 over the past ten years. This tax is paid by her husband, whose salary is considerably larger than his wife's earnings. She has invested the $4,000 each year in three different equity funds which have averaged a 22% return annually. Her income-splitting savings fund now totals over $140,000, and the average annual return is now higher than her annual income from writing.

This income-splitting technique is possible only if the lower income spouse is self-employed or earning a considerable amount of investment income and must pay all or a portion of tax in quarterly instalments. The technique does not work if the lower income spouse is employed and receives a paycheque where income tax is deducted at source.

The important thing with this and other income-splitting arrangements is to be able to trace the source of the funds that were used to acquire income-earning assets. For example, the lower income spouse should write cheques for the purchase of investments from the same bank account to which his or her work-related income is deposited. The higher income spouse should not make temporary loans to the lower income spouse for the purchase of these investments, unless they are *bona fide,* well-documented loans that bear interest at the commercial rate and are repaid. Better still, the lower income spouse might consider taking out a short-term loan from the bank to buy the investments.

2. Keep Refundable Child Tax Credit and Other Amounts Separate If the lower income spouse is the recipient of refundable child tax credits or any other type of tax refund from the government, these should be deposited directly by this spouse to his or her own bank account rather than being co-mingled with family funds. The lower income spouse can then use these particular funds to advance through the seven steps of the financial security formula and subsequently make other investments. The same advice applies to any other amounts that the lower income spouse might earn or receive directly. These could include in-heritances, gifts from parents or other relatives, unemployment insurance payments (whether or not they are received on account of maternity leave), and family allowance payments if these cheques are not used to fund the post-secondary education of your children.

3. Setting Up a Spousal RRSP Spousal RRSPs are one of the few income-splitting techniques encouraged under the tax law. With a spousal RRSP, you contribute to an RRSP of which your spouse is the annuitant (the person who will receive and be taxed on the resulting RRSP retirement income). However, you get to deduct the contribution from your income.

Spousal RRSPs are valuable in that they can be used to provide your spouse with a level of retirement income that he or she otherwise may not have been able to generate. Also, instead of having this income taxed in your hands, it will now be taxed in your spouse's hands at a lower rate, which will increase the total amount of income that you and your spouse will have on retirement.

For example, assume that $1,000 of retirement income would be taxed in your hands at 40%. If spousal RRSP contributions are made instead, then the $1,000 is taxed in your spouse's hands at 25%. After-tax income jumps to $750 from $600, a 25% increase. To generate that $1,000 in twenty-five years' time, you need to contribute as little as $500 now to a spousal RRSP that earns 12% compounded annually.

With the higher RRSP limits, you may now be able to make sizeable spousal RRSP contributions and still contribute significant amounts to your own RRSP. RRSPs are discussed in detail in Chapter 6.

4. Use Spousal Borrowing If you intend to borrow for investment purposes, you might consider borrowing jointly with your lower income spouse. Each of you would repay your respective portions of the loan plus interest from your own funds and include the appropriate amount of earnings in each of your incomes for tax purposes. If the higher income spouse pays any of the lower income spouse's interest on the loan or repays any part of the lower income spouse's principal, the attribution rules will apply and the income-splitting objective will not be met.

Better still, the lower income spouse could borrow on his or her own account, and, if necessary, the higher income spouse would guarantee the loan. In this case, the lower income spouse must pay all interest and repay the principal from his or her own funds; otherwise the attribution rules will apply. All the resulting investment income would be taxed in the hands of the lower income spouse.

5. Interest on Interest Not Attributed Since interest on interest, or investment income earned on income already earned, is not attributable, you may want to consider doing all your investing in the name of your spouse, even though the attribution rules will apply. The income earned on all capital amounts transferred to the spouse will be taxable in your hands, but any income earned on the attributed income will be considered to be earned in the hands of the lower income spouse. It may take a little bookkeeping to keep the two classes of income separate, but the savings in a few years could be sizeable.

For example, assume that you are currently earning income of $3,000 at 12% on capital of $25,000. You put the capital in your spouse's name so that he or she earns the $3,000. In the first year, the entire $3,000 is taxed in your hands and in each succeeding year $3,000 will be taxed in your hands under attribution rules. However, each year the $3,000 is segregated into separate investments in your spouse's name. In the second year, your spouse earns $360 on the $3,000 (income at 12% on the first year's income of $3,000), which has been segregated. At the beginning of the third year, another $3,000 has been segregated for a total of $6,000, plus there is the previous year's earnings of $360, assuming the spouse did not pay any tax on the amount. So, in the third year, your spouse earns $763 (12% of $6,360). This scenario repeats itself every year with $3,000 being segregated each year.

In the tenth year, your spouse earns $5,319. Assuming that the

Year	Taxed in Your Hands	Taxed in Spouse's hands	Spouse Accumulates ($25,000 +)
1	$3,000	0	$ 3,000
2	$3,000	$ 360	$ 6,360
3	$3,000	$ 763	$10,123
4	$3,000	$1,215	$14,338
.			.
.			
.			.
9	$3,000	$4,428	$44,328
10	$3,000	$5,319	$52,647

income is taxable, that he or she earns no other income and the full $1,000 investment income deduction is available, he or she would be taxed for the first time in this year. The tax payable, however, would be only about $6 in most provinces, using 1987 rates. Earnings on the original $25,000 are still being attributed to you each year, and you would have to pay taxes on the $3,000 out of your other income, but this allows a faster compounding of income in your spouse's hands and allows him or her to eventually earn more income, more quickly. It should be noted that for several years during this program, you would be losing the married status deduction, which does not result in any adverse tax consequences. You should also bear in mind that at the end of ten years, the entire $77,641 ($25,000 plus $52,647 minus tax of $6) belongs to your spouse.

6. If You Own a Business If your spouse is employed in your business, you may pay him or her a salary as long as it is reasonable in relation to the duties performed by the spouse. The same condition applies to a salary paid to your spouse by a corporation that you control. The salary is not attributed to you. If your spouse is a shareholder, there may be other methods of getting income into his or her hands that you should discuss with a professional adviser.

If you and your spouse operate a business together in partnership, income from the business may be split between you, with no attribution, based on your respective "contributions to the business." In determining whether this allocation is reasonable, the tax authorities will look at relevant contributions to the business, including capital contributions, the labour of each spouse in the business and the special expertise of either spouse essential to the operation of the business.

In addition, if the higher income spouse provides a loan to the lower income spouse to start a business or expand an existing business, there is no attribution of any resulting business income. The higher income spouse could also guarantee a third-party loan to the lower income spouse and/or pay the interest on such a loan.

Under the rules introduced in 1985, it has become difficult to split income with a spouse through an investment corporation. However, if you are the primary shareholder of a corporation that earns mainly business income, it may be relatively easy to implement a tax-reducing income-splitting program by involving your spouse and other family members in the ownership of the corporation. Quality professional advice should be sought from a lawyer or a chartered accountant.

A Word about Ownership of Transferred Property Please take note that any assets transferred to your spouse, including by means of a spousal RRSP, as well as any income earned in the spouse's hands on these assets, belong irrevocably to him or her. The only way for you to regain ownership of the assets is for your spouse to transfer ownership back to you, for the assets to be awarded to you on the breakdown of the marriage or for you to inherit the assets on the death of your spouse. Family law legislation in many provinces insists on a fifty-fifty split of most assets (all assets in some provinces) on the permanent breakdown of a marriage. So, there is little point holding back on an income-splitting program if your only concern is the permanent loss of control over your assets.

Should You Consider Buying a Vacation Home as One of Your Investments under the $500,000 Lifetime Capital Gains Exemption?

Deciding whether to purchase a vacation home, such as a cottage, four-season chalet or Florida condo, does not involve the same investment considerations as deciding whether or not to buy a home – not even if you are thinking of acquiring the vacation home before you acquire your principal home. There are two major differences.

First, you will not be living in the vacation home on a full-time basis. Essentially, it is an alternative to a vacation of a different type or an alternative to renting a vacation home. Any decision to purchase a vacation property should be approached from this point of view.

Second, any gain you realize on the vacation home when it is your family's second home might be taxed as a capital gain. However, such gains, no matter where the property is located, are, at the present time, included under your $500,000 capital gains exemption. Remember, however, that you could be subject to a foreign capital gains tax if the home is located in another country.

Generally, it is more expensive – that is, a poorer investment – to own a vacation home and use it periodically than it is to rent a comparable property and use it for the same period. Only if the property escalates in value substantially and quickly might you be better off owning it.

Nevertheless, many people do purchase vacation homes. Some make the purchase with the intention of the vacation property becoming one of their two retirement homes, and therefore look on it as prudent retirement planning. Often, they will treat it as almost a pure investment for the first few years of ownership, renting it out for most of the vacation season and spending perhaps only two or three weeks in it themselves. This type of arrangement can make sense, assuming that the two or three weeks you spend using the property are in lieu of spending money on a vacation elsewhere. However, you then become a landlord with all the attendant problems it may involve, not the least of which is the fact that your rental property is perhaps a few hundred kilometers or more from your home. You then have no easy, inexpensive way of keeping an eye on it or of ensuring that it remains in good shape.

Sometimes Buying a Vacation Home Makes Sense This is not to say that you should discard the idea of buying a vacation home. They can make sense in some situations.

Planning Profile

After looking around semi-seriously for a number of years, Alan and Barbara Segal finally bought an older cottage situated in a desirable area north of Toronto. After modernizing the plumbing, adding two small bedrooms, generally fixing the place up and overhauling the boat that came with the property, almost all of which Alan did himself, they had sunk about $50,000 into the cottage.

If they had invested that $50,000 elsewhere, the Segals thought they could have made 10% on it after taxes, or $5,000 a year. Plus, they figured their annual cottage expenses to be in the region of $1,500, for a total of $6,500 annually.

However, when they bought the cottage, Alan and Barbara arranged a deal with neighbours to rent it to them for about $1,500 a year. The neighbours would get two or three weeks plus a couple of weekends. The arrangement still works out perfectly and the Segals have never felt like landlords.

They then totalled up what they would have spent on vacations if they had not owned the cottage. They estimated this conservatively at $3,000 and then threw in another $500 for the weekends, which was probably very conservative for the twelve to fifteen weekends the Segals spent at the cottage.

That left $1,500 to account for in appreciation of the cottage. However, this is only a 3% rise in value each year and they knew that cottages in the area had been increasing in value at about 5% or 6% a year for the past few years.

Alan and Barbara's cottage has proved to be a good investment for four specific reasons:

- They bought intelligently, got a good price and keep costs to a minimum by doing almost all repairs and maintenance work themselves.
- They bought in an area close enough to the city so that

prices should continue to increase at a rate above the average for vacation properties.

- They have a sweetheart rental deal with a neighbour that is just about the same as winning $1,500 a year in a lottery, minus the small amount of tax they pay on this rental income.
- They use the cottage to the maximum from ice-out to ice-in, as an alternative to "vacationing" in the city on weekends or taking extended vacations elsewhere. In fact, they would probably spend in excess of $3,500 during these months on "vacations" if they did not have the cottage.

The Segals now plan to winterize the cottage themselves so it can be used as a ski chalet. They figure they can do this over the next two years for about $5,000. Performing the same alternative vacation calculations, that would mean spending at least $500 a year on skiing accommodation to make the winterizing economically justifiable. However, one three-day weekend for the whole family at a ski resort would set them back well in excess of $500, so the winterizing would certainly seem to be worthwhile.

Buying the Right Vacation Home Is Not Easy There are many available in every area imaginable. If possible, you should rent in various locations for a couple of years, do all your homework and then buy carefully. Remember that you might be able to get in on the renter side, not the landlord side, of a sweetheart rental deal that could prove to be the wiser investment alternative over the long run.

Leveraging Your Investments

Borrowing to invest is certainly not for everybody, but a few people may want to give it some consideration once they reach Step 6 in the financial security formula.

Aside from how your investments perform, there are really only two things that affect your ultimate rate of return when you borrow to invest: your after-tax interest expense and the amount of tax payable on your investment income (the word *income* as used in this book includes capital gains). Thus, if you are paying interest at 12% and your tax rate is 37.5% (federal rate of 25% plus provincial rate of 50% times 25%), your out-of-pocket, after-tax interest expense is 7.5% (interest paid at 12% less tax saving of 4.5% (37.5% of 12%). Similarly, if the investment earns income at 12% and the full amount is taxable at your marginal rate, your after-tax return is 7.5%. You would break even on this investment, so there would be no point in investing.

If interest is deductible, it is deductible in full from income, and therefore your tax saving on the interest expense is always your marginal rate times the amount of interest paid. However, remember that dividends are taxed at a lower rate than interest and employment income, and that the first $500,000 of capital gains realized after 1984 (phased in through to 1990) is exempt from tax.

For example, assume that you manage to earn Canadian dividend income at the rate of 12% and your tax rate is still 37.5%. Your after-tax return on the dividends is 10% but could be slightly higher or lower depending on the province in which you live. In this case, your after-tax profit on the investment would be 2.5% (10% minus 7.5%). If you realize a capital gain at the rate of 12% on your investment, no tax is payable assuming your $500,000 capital gain exemption is available. In this case, your after-tax profit is 4.5% (12% minus 7.5%). These numbers are summarized in Table 9.1.

Table 9.1: Rates of Return on Leveraged Investments

	Interest	Dividends	Exempt Capital Gains
Income	12 %	12 %	12 %
Less: Tax	4.5	2	0
Profit net of tax	7.5	10	12
Less: After-tax cost of borrowing	7.5	7.5	7.5
Profit net of tax and cost of borrowing	0	2.5%	4.5%

Investment income: 12%
Federal tax rate: 25% plus Provincial tax rate: 12.5% (50% of 25%)
Funds borrowed at: 12%

Your "real" after-tax return on these investments is much more impressive. Since you are using someone else's money, only the earnings themselves suffer the effects of inflation. For example, assume that you borrow $1,000 at 12%. The loan is repaid in full at the end of the year along with $120 in interest, or $75 in after-tax interest. You earn dividends of $120 by the end of the year. Your net return after taxes on the dividends (tax rate is 37.5%) is $100 and, after deducting the after-tax cost of borrowing ($75), your after-tax net return is $25 on the investment (see Table 9.1). You are, in effect, investing $75 (after-tax interest) to earn an after-tax profit of $25, which is an after-tax return of 33⅓%.

Does this mean that everybody should borrow as much as possible to earn these annual 33⅓% after-tax returns? It certainly is how many people get rich. It is also how many get ulcers and poor at the same time. Their investments perform wretchedly, and they cannot afford to comfortably repay the loan out of other sources of income. Also bear in mind that if you can earn interest at 12%, dividends on preferred shares more than likely will be in the 7% to 10% range. Nevertheless, there are several situations where you might consider borrowing for investment purposes.

Conservative Borrowing within Your Income-Splitting Program

You may want to borrow to implement an additional aspect of your income-splitting program. You will have made it to Step 6 in the financial security formula, and, in addition, you will have made spousal RRSP contributions and the lower income spouse will have already maximized his or her $1,000 Canadian investment income deduction.

However, you might feel that your income-splitting needs a further shot in the arm, which means that the lower income spouse must improve the return on his or her investments. The couple in the planning profile outlined below do not expect to run into any problems funding the education of their children; they have moved into Steps 6 and 7 in the financial security formula; and they are prepared to take a certain amount of risk with some of the income they now earn.

Planning Profile

Gail Omoto, who just turned forty, has been out of the work force for a number of years, but re-entered it three years ago and has a well-paying job. However, over her working life, she will earn considerably less than Bob, her husband, and is therefore the lower income spouse. Gail and Bob have determined that each year she has $1,000 of before-tax employment income available for investing. This would amount to $600 after taxes of $400 are paid (40% tax rate applied to $1,000). She has a choice of either investing the after-tax amount of $600 each year or using her income to pay the interest on a loan and investing the proceeds of the loan. The interest on the loan is deductible, so she is able to pay interest of $1,000 annually, consisting of her $600 after-tax employment income and her $400 tax saving generated when she deducts the $1,000 interest expense from income. This interest expense does not reduce the amount of income eligible for her $1,000 investment income deduction because of the nature of the investments acquired with the borrowed funds.

In an attempt to increase her investment return, Gail Omoto invests in an equity investment fund, which produces predominantly capital gains and which invests exclusively in foreign investments. She has not used any of her $500,000 capital gains exemption so that any capital gains on her investment will not be taxable. Occasionally she receives dividends from the fund, representing dividends from foreign securities, but these are ignored in the calculations below. However, the fact that she does occasionally receive the dividends ensures that any interest expense she incurs to enable her to purchase units of the fund will be deductible for tax purposes.

Gail borrows at 12% and, after allowing for any front-end load fees and other expenses, the fund earns 15% annually, all of which is a capital gain. Early in 1987 there were more than seventy equity funds that earned in excess of 15% annually, on average, over the preceding ten-year period, and at least a dozen of these earned over 20%. So 15% is certainly not an unreasonable return.

Gail is able to borrow $8,333 at an interest rate of 12%. She then invests the $8,333 in the equity fund and leaves it there for ten years, paying interest on the loan the whole time, but not repaying any principal. She borrows half the $8,333 from Bob, but since she pays the interest from her own funds, the attribution rules do not apply. She borrows the other half from the bank, pledging all the unit certificates of the equity fund with her bank manager as security for the loan. Usually borrowers are required to pay off some principal on loans as well as interest, but since she is otherwise a first-rate credit risk, the manager has agreed that she need only pay the interest on the loan.

By borrowing and investing in the equity fund, Gail's units in the fund are worth about $33,700 at the end of the tenth year. After paying off the bank loan of $8,333, she has accumulated almost $25,400. If the Omotos had invested her $600 of after-tax employment income in the fund at the beginning of each year for ten years, Gail would have accumulated only about $14,000 at the end of the tenth year. This is about $11,400 less than she has accumulated by using the $600 each year as interest on the investment loan.

The longer the Omotos keep Gail's investment leveraged and the higher the return in the fund, the better off they will be compared to directly investing her annual after-tax employment income. In fact, when Gail borrows at 12%, the earnings rate on the equity fund must drop to 7% or less before she would be worse off borrowing.

What Are the Risks? First, she might not invest in the fund long enough to take advantage of historical trends. Investment funds have outperformed many other investments over the long term: that is, at least ten years. However, she may invest in the fund at a peak in the market cycle and see her units decline in value by say 10% in the first year. In the second year, they rebound by about 11%, but, unfortunately, she must cash her units to fund an emergency at the end of the second year. She discovers that her equity fund units exactly cover the amount of the loans and she has nothing left for the emergency. Using the cash method, she would have about $1,200 after cashing her units.

Second, the bank could decide to call her loan at any time, despite the existence of the collateral. Her financial position will then depend on the size of the loan and the accumulated gain in the equity fund. If the loan is not called for at least several years and her gain is substantial, she will in most cases be further ahead using the investment loan technique than she would buying units annually with her after-tax employment income. If the loan is called early and the price of the units is depressed, she would be in the same position as if she had cashed the units early herself, as in the case outlined above.

Third, interest rates could increase, perhaps dramatically. Bob and Gail have three options if this occurs. Gail can reduce the principal on her loans so that she is still paying $1,000 in interest each year. For example, if interest rates climb to 18% from 12%, she could reduce the loan principal from $8,333 to $5,555, and her $1,000 would still pay the interest. However, this would mean selling units of the equity fund, which reduces the total return she expects over the long term. She could also pay the additional interest – $500 in this case – which costs her $300 in after-tax dollars. This second option is more attractive in most circumstances. If interest rates are high only temporarily, she will be back on track in a short time paying 12% again. If interest rates do not go down, then inflation also will be high and wages will be increasing quickly enough to finance the higher interest expense. (In fact, using leverage extensively is one way many people stay ahead of inflation.) The third option is to sell everything, repay the loans and use the funds to buy long-term interest-bearing investments. This may look attractive, but remember that the interest will be taxable, and it is not easy to earn positive real returns with interest when we have double-digit inflation. Only when interest rates decline again will a substantial real return be earned.

Fourth, Bob and Gail run the risk of history not repeating itself. There is no guarantee that equity investment funds will continue, on average, to perform as they have over the past ten years. Markets may go into a massive slump and the fund will only break even over a ten-year period. If Gail borrows, she will have nothing at the end of ten years, whereas by using the cash method, she will have $6,000 ($600 of after-tax employment income each year times ten years).

Finally, there is the extremely slight risk that the fund's assets will be "mismanaged" to the point where they evaporate. Gail's units will be worthless, unless some restitution is made, and she will owe the bank the amount of her loan. The bank will undoubtedly want her to begin repaying principal and interest immediately.

In conclusion, if you borrow to finance your investing or to gain a certain amount of leverage, you must be prepared to lose more than just the amount you pay in interest. Therefore, you should borrow with the expectation of reaping an attractive return to compensate for the risk. Most taxpayers find out relatively quickly what their risk tolerance is when they combine borrowing with equity investing. Don't be afraid to withdraw from the investments if you find that you overestimated your risk tolerance level. Often this is a sign that you are about to begin losing money, for no other reason than you are too emotionally distraught to make sensible investment decisions.

10

Seventh Step: Funding Your Children's Post-Secondary Education

This final step in the financial security formula should not, in theory, be reached by many average Canadians. That's not because you won't be helping your children with their college education. It's just unlikely that you will have sufficient income available before the time your children reach college age to address this goal after having achieved the other, higher-priority goals. Nevertheless, many families take a stab at funding their children's education, often before attempting Steps 3, 4, 5 and 6, by habitually putting away family allowance payments in the names of their children. This is an admirable practice, but only as long as it is not hindering you from purchasing your first home. But on the whole, your family will be better off if you follow the steps in the formula in numerical order. You will accumulate more wealth over the long term and have more flexibility to meet a variety of financial needs, including the college expenses of your children.

Looking at Step 7 from a different perspective, the only reason for putting assets in the names of your children is to improve the return on investments by eliminating tax. But you are not paying tax on your investments in Steps 2 through 6, so you won't be any further ahead to undertake Step 7 before the others. As well it was noted earlier that funding your children's education may rank high on your list of financial priorities emotionally, but from an economic point of view, it comes in dead last. There are at least two reasons for this: lack of financial and investment flexibility, and loss of control over assets transferred to the children.

It is not easy to find two people who agree on how their children's university or college education should be financed and who is responsible for the financing. Some feel that they owe it to their children to cover every expense for however many years it takes to get a degree or degrees, usually because they believe that the child will perform much better if relieved of all financial worry. Others think that the child should be totally responsible for funding his or her education through personal earnings, loans and scholarships. Most strike a position somewhere in between, often because their relatively limited resources give them no choice. Three or four years of university or college can be expensive, especially if your children are not living at home. Most families simply do not and will not have the savings to completely finance one child's education, let alone two or three children.

Sources of Education Funding

Once your children reach university age, you will discover that a variety of sources can be tapped for financing their education. The most important source, although not necessarily the largest, should be the children's own earnings and savings, followed by any student loans that they can arrange, and of course scholarships, grants and bursaries if they happen to be available. There is no reason why your children should not take as much financial responsibility for their education as is reasonable under the circumstances. And student loans, which are interest-free while the student remains in school, have been one of the great bargains over the past two decades.

The next most important, and in some cases the largest, source of financing for your children's education is the funds you have specifically saved over the preceding ten or twenty years. These may result from an income-splitting program with your child, several techniques of which are the subject of this chapter. If not enough funding is available from these sources, you would then turn to your day-to-day earnings to make up any shortfall.

These four sources – child's earnings, student loans, education savings and day-to-day earnings – should, for most average Canadians, provide all the funds necessary to see their children through three or four years of university or college. However, if you have more than one child in university at the same time, and none of the children are living at home, you may have to search for other sources of financing.

The first place to look is your additional retirement saving (Step 6) or your contingency fund (Step 5), if you have built one up. If you have several children close to one another in age, this might be one very good reason for developing a large contingency fund. You also might consider a short-term loan for lump-sum expenses such as tuition or residence fees. However, if you cannot comfortably repay the loan over less than twelve months, you may then have to think about borrowing against your home (mortgaging it) or withdrawing some of your savings from your RRSPs.

Since the education expenses are limited by the amount of time your children are in school, and as soon as they graduate your finances will be much healthier, you should first consider mortgaging your home, which is simply a cheap form of borrowing, using your house as collateral. As a pure investment decision, you would mortgage your home if the interest rate were less than the rate you are earning in the RRSP, and withdraw funds from the RRSP if the mortgage rate were higher than the RRSP earnings rate. However, over the long term, you could be worse off withdrawing funds from your RRSP since you lose the tax-sheltered status by removing the funds. Later, when you have the cash available, you cannot make up for the amounts withdrawn and regain that tax-sheltered advantage.

Mortgaging your home or withdrawing funds from RRSPs to fund your children's education can possibly jeopardize your family's future, since you are spending a portion of your retirement fund. Many families will want to make the sacrifice, while others will draw the line at some point and expect their children to contribute more to their education. Hence the importance of sticking to the financial security formula and making it up to Step 6 or 7 as soon as possible so that it is unlikely you will be put in this position.

Your Kids Can Earn Tax-Free Income Too

As you have seen, the primary investment tactic used in Steps 2 through to 6 is to improve your after-tax real return on investments by eliminating tax. Paying down the mortgage on your home is the same as earning tax-free interest. No tax is payable on your net investment in an RRSP (i.e., the amount invested net of your tax refund). And no tax is payable on the first $1,000 of Canadian interest income earned and up to $500,000 of capital gains. Similarly, the emphasis on funding your children's education is to eliminate tax on any investment income.

How important is eliminating tax to the financing of your children's education? If your marginal tax rate is 40%, you have to earn $2,500 to finance tuition of $1,500, because first you must pay tax of $1,000 on the $2,500. If you eliminate the tax element, you only have to earn $1,500 to finance the tuition of $1,500. Similarly, the cost of educating your children drops dramatically if you can eliminate all tax payable on investments earmarked as education funding.

If you are already using all your $1,000 investment income deduction, it is virtually impossible for you to invest in low-risk interest-bearing securities and not pay tax. However, if your children earn that interest income, it is unlikely they will pay any tax because their income is too low for it to be taxable. In 1987, any person can earn up to about $4,200 ($5,200 if income includes $1,000 of Canadian interest) and not pay any federal or provincial tax. A college student can earn more since he or she can deduct tuition fees from income for tax purposes, as well as the $50 a month education allowance. There is not the same problem with capital gains, since both you and your spouse are each entitled to the lifetime $500,000 exemption. It is unlikely that the average Canadian couple will exceed this limit.

There is one major obstacle to having your children earn interest income that you otherwise would have earned, and several drawbacks to such planning.

The Attribution Rules

Rules similar to those that discourage income splitting with your spouse also apply to income splitting with your children. Actually the rules apply to income splitting with any child under the age of eighteen. Under these attribution rules, all interest and dividend income earned on funds transferred by you in any manner to your child is taxed in your hands and not in your child's hands, even though that income may legally belong to the child. A transfer includes a gift, a loan or a sale, whether made directly or indirectly through a trust or another third party. Capital gains are not subject to the attribution rules and the rules cease to apply in the year a child turns eighteen, even in respect of income that may have been earned before this date but did not have to be reported for tax purposes.

It no longer makes economic sense to lend money to a child trust, which used to be one of the more common ways of having children earn income that otherwise would have been earned by the parent. If such a loan is made, interest must be paid each year or within thirty days of the end of the year, and the loan must bear interest at a rate no lower than the commercial rate in effect at the time the loan was made or the prescribed rate at that time. (As you may remember, the *prescribed rate* is the interest rate payable on late tax payments, or the interest payable by the federal government after April 30 on tax refunds.) The prescribed rate is revised every three months to reflect changes in current interest rates.

Although the restrictions on loans made to child trusts make it difficult to transfer large sums to a child, there are several other methods of placing assets in your children's hands. Before discussing five income-splitting ideas, you should be aware of two specific limitations in any income-splitting program.

The Drawbacks of Income Splitting with Your Children

First, you must bear in mind that for any income-splitting program to be effective, assets must be transferred to the child, which means that you might lose control over the assets and over the resulting income. This may not be a problem if you can keep the child in the dark about investments that are actually in the child's name. In most cases, this is not difficult at least until the child enters university and begins to use the funds. However, you may be forced to give the game away earlier if the children's income becomes high enough to be taxable, and they have to fill out and sign a tax return. Thus you might either have to raise responsible children who won't blow their college money on a new sports car, or set up the child's investments so that they are locked-in until specific dates, such as the day tuition must be paid each September.

One way to avoid this potential problem, if you think it might be one, is to implement a trust, with your children as beneficiaries and you as one of the trustees who controls distributions from the trust. It is beyond the scope of this book to discuss trusts in detail, but child trusts are relatively simple to understand and to manage. In fact, you can probably put one together yourself with the aid of a self-help book, or a lawyer or trust company can put one together for a one-time-only fee and you can manage it for the next twenty years or so.

Second, it is not always an easy matter in this country to make investments in the name of a person under the age of eighteen, since contracts with minor children are not legally binding. However, with a little work, you should be able to find a willing banker, broker or insurance company. Most institutions have no problems with savings accounts set up in the name of a minor, and there should generally be no problem with other investments, such as Canada Savings Bonds or GICs, since the institution is not expecting the child to fulfil a legal obligation such as paying back money on a loan or paying for the investment sometime after it is actually purchased.

One other slight drawback is the loss of the dependant's deduction if the child's income is too high. Dependent children are allowed to earn a certain amount each year before the dependant's deduction is reduced or eliminated. From 1987 to 1989, the dependant's deduction for all children (whether under the age of eighteen or over the age of seventeen) will be reduced considerably, so the loss of the deduction will pose less of a hardship. To compensate for this reduction, the amount that a child can earn without the dependant's exemption being affected will increase significantly over the same period. Note that the income used to determine the size of the dependant's deduction is the net income shown on the tax return form, which is the child's income after deducting tuition, the $500 employment expense deduction and Canada Pension Plan and Unemployment Insurance premiums paid, if any.

Five Income-Splitting Techniques and Investments

1. Investing Family Allowance Payments Historically, the tax authorities have not applied the attribution rules to income earned by a child on family allowance payments that are placed in the child's name. Thus, you should consider a program where you deposit these monthly payments in a bank account in the child's name. You also might be able to find a money market fund that will accept monthly deposits of your family allowance cheques. As the account or the fund increases in size, you would purchase investments with a more attractive return. The best investment would be equity funds over the long term, especially since you (or the child) will not be using some of the savings for as long as twenty years. However, you could also acquire equity funds in your own name and not lose control of the assets (this is discussed in the previous chapter), so you would purchase equal amounts of strips and CSBs. If you think interest rates are relatively high, buy the long-term strips before the CSBs. You might want to weight those purchases made before the child reaches the age of ten in favour of strips, since you can pick a specific maturity and then not have to worry about reinvesting. Family allowance payments currently are less than $400 a year. Thus, you may only be able to acquire specific investments every two or three or four years, although CSBs currently come in denominations as low as $100.

If you wish to establish some control over the child's assets you could open the bank account "in trust" for the child, which gives you control over disbursing amounts to the child. This prevents the child from gaining access to the funds until he or she turns eighteen, the age of legal majority.

In theory, the child should be filing a tax return reporting the income earned on the investments, but this is not really necessary until the child's income is at a level where tax is payable by the child. However, you should keep track of the child's net income for tax purposes, since at some point your dependant's exemption for the child will be reduced or eliminated. If a tax return is filed for the child, you can sign it on the child's behalf until he or she turns eighteen, which keeps the child from knowing about any accumulated funds until at least shortly before he or she begins post-secondary schooling.

One drawback to this plan is that tax is payable on the family allowance payments by the spouse who claims the child as a dependant in his or her tax return, which means that the tax payment must come from other income.

You might want to investigate a more risky plan where the family allowance payments are used as interest on an investment loan. This is discussed in more detail below.

2. Putting Aside Your Child's Own Earnings Another easy technique for placing income in your child's hands is to have the child save all his or her earnings from whatever source, except amounts paid by you as an allowance or for chores. You would then give the child a matching amount. You would obviously want to extract a promise from the child not to touch the savings until they are needed for post-secondary education. For this plan to work, the child would have to deposit the amounts in the bank in his or her name when received. To keep the child from having access to the amounts, the child could make the deposits to the family allowance bank account that was opened "in trust" for the child.

With this technique, you cannot act as the child's banker and distribute the matching funds when you feel like it, since the tax authorities would claim that you are simply returning the child's earnings to him or her. Another way to keep the child's hands off the funds is to arrange for the purchase of long-term investments that mature or are cashable only when the child needs the money for school. It is unlikely that any financial institution would allow a child under eighteen to borrow money using the long-term securities as collateral.

It will probably not be until your child is at least ten years old that he or she is earning any income. This leaves only eight to twelve years before the funds are needed for the child's college education. You might consider investing the first $1,000 in five-year GICs if interest rates are attractive, and the next $1,000 in a money market fund. You would then repeat the cycle, bearing in mind that the maturity date of the GICs will have to coincide with the date the funds will be needed.

3. Acquiring Deferred Income Securities The child attribution rules cease to apply in the year the child turns eighteen years old. Therefore, you could purchase deferred income securities in the child's name, so long as the child does not receive the interest or recognize it for tax purposes until the year he or she turns eighteen. However, the three-year accrual rules inhibit you from implementing this type of income-splitting program until the year in which the child turns fifteen years old, since the interest being earned on such debt obligations must be reported every three years. The anniversary date for tax purposes is considered to be three years after December 31 of the year the security was issued, and every three years after that.

Thus, if you think your child is going to enter university in four years, when he or she turns nineteen, and that he or she will attend for four years after that, you could buy four different GICs or strips with four-, five-, six- and seven-year maturities. Shop around to get the best rate. Any accumulated interest, plus principal, would be payable to the child and the interest earned would be taxed in his or her hands.

As an alternative, if you have sufficient funds available, you could lend an amount to a child who is at least fifteen years old, with the income earned on that amount being used for educational purposes. For example, you might lend the child $20,000 and the child would purchase the four different GICs for $5,000 each. The interest at maturity of each GIC would belong to the child and be used for college expenses. The $20,000 loan would be repaid to you in $5,000 instalments in each year a GIC matured. The attribution rules would not apply because no income on the loaned funds would be recognized for tax purposes until the child is at least eighteen years old.

4. Should Registered Education Savings Plans (RESPs) Be Used? Registered Education Savings Plans (RESPs) are not strongly recommended because of the risk involved. Essentially, you contribute after-tax funds (no deduction from income is permitted) to a RESP, and earnings in the RESP accumulate free of tax while funds remain in the plan. When your child enters university or another qualifying post-secondary institution, an amount is paid each year for three or four years from the RESP to the child, part of which is taxable income to the child. The catch is that if your child does not pursue a post-secondary education, you receive only your contributions back from the plan, not the earnings on them for the period that your cash was in the RESP. Hence, those children who do go to university benefit at the expense of those who do not.

It may be possible for another family member or even yourself to be named as the beneficiary of the RESP and become entitled to the RESP payments, if the original beneficiary does not attend university or college. If you are positive that someone will use the scholarship funds, you might want to consider a RESP, especially now that changes to the attribution rules have made child trusts impracticable. RESPs are most beneficial if begun when your child is very young. However, most parents have higher financial priorities at this point, such as buying their first home, paying down the mortgage or beginning to save for their retirement.

In general, RESPs are too risky for any average Canadian to consider. If you have the funds available when your children are quite young, you would be better off investing the funds yourself in an investment fund where you can realize capital gains tax-free under your $500,000 capital gains exemption.

5. No Attribution on Capital Gains Realized by Your Children As noted above, there is no attribution on capital gains realized by a child on assets transferred by you. Therefore, you may want to consider buying capital property in your child's name. However, you and your spouse each have a lifetime $500,000 capital gains exemption. If you do not expect to exhaust the full $500,000 ($1 million between the both of you), there is no point in relinquishing control of capital assets to your children when no tax will be payable on capital gains in any case. Such funds would be invested in an equity fund, if you planned to leave the funds there for at least five years. You will be able to invest in any equity fund, not just the ones qualifying as RRSP investments.

How Much Can Your Child Accumulate – Is It Really Worthwhile?

A surprising amount can accumulate if you put all family allowance payments in the name of the child and have the child bank his or her earnings as shown in the following example.

Planning Profile

Sheila Barrett is a single parent who treats the family allowance cheques as found money and has banked every one in her child's name. By the time her five-year-old daughter, Anne, is eighteen, she expects to have more than $20,000 accumulated, based on the assumption that the payments will average $400 each year (these are actually indexed so she will probably receive more) and interest will be earned at an average rate of 10% a year. If she adds a bit on to allow for the family allowance payments being indexed, and she reimburses Anne for earnings put towards her education, Sheila thinks she may have close to $30,000 available by the time her daughter begins college. If inflation averages 6%, this $30,000 will be worth about $10,500 in today's dollars, or well over $3,000 a year for a four-year university course, if the funds continue to earn tax-free interest at 10%. If this is combined with the daughter's summer earnings and student loans, most if not all the financial pressure to continually supply money for tuition, room and board, and entertainment should be eliminated for those four years.

Family Allowance Payment Investment Loans

If you are relatively confident about achieving a comfortable level of financial security and about reaching at least Step 6 in the formula, you may want to consider another option for those family allowance payments. Instead of buying CSBs or strips or money market fund units, you could use the monthly payment as interest on an investment loan, much the same as Gail did in the profile presented in Chapter 9. You would buy units in an equity fund – probably in your own name, assuming you were not going to use up your $500,000 capital gains exemption. If this exemption is in danger, put the equity fund units in the name of the child. Any resulting capital gains are not attributable to you, and they are not taxable in the hands of the child who has his or her own $500,000 capital gains exemption. Bear in mind, however, that the investment will belong to the child and you could lose control of it.

The higher income spouse – that is, the spouse with the higher marginal tax rate for the period when family allowance payments are being received – should undertake this program since more funds will be accumulated.

Assume the following:

- Family allowance payments are $32 a month over an eighteen-year period.
- The mother's tax rate is 30%, while the father's is 40%, so he undertakes the program.
- He can borrow at 13% and pay only interest (not principal) on the loan.
- The equity fund earns 16% compounded annually.

At a 13% borrowing rate, he can borrow $7.69 for each dollar of interest. And since the interest is deductible, he can pay $32 a month plus his tax saving of $21.33, for a total interest payment over the year of about $640. This means he can borrow slightly over $4,900. If the fund earns 16% a year, he will accumulate about $66,000 at the end of eighteen years after repaying the loan. If he had invested the family allowance payments in the fund, he would accumulate only about $35,000 after eighteen years, which is $31,000 less than using the investment loan technique. If the equity fund earns 18% annually, the difference between the two methods is about $49,000 ($92,000 minus $43,000), because she is not able to borrow as much.

If the wife had undertaken the program, she would accumulate only about $57,000, which is $9,000 ($66,000 minus $57,000) less than the husband accumulates if the fund earns 16% annually.

Before implementing the investment loan plan, you should consider carefully the five risks which Gail faced in the profile presented in Chapter 9:

1. Interest rates may go up.
2. You may have to put an end to the program after only a year or two, at which time the market may be depressed.

3. You may have to repay your loan sooner than you expected.
4. History may not repeat itself, and the rate of return on the equity fund will be much lower than the interest rate on the loan.
5. In the worst case, the fund might be mismanaged to the point where your units are more or less worthless.

Also, you should bear in mind that tax is payable on the family allowance payments by the spouse who claims the child as a dependant.

11

The Only Investments You Need

There are hundreds of investment products on the market, almost all of which are directed to the extremely knowledgeable and, for the most part, wealthy person who usually has access to full-time professional advisers. So if you want your investing to be simple, straightforward and with a decidedly conservative, low-risk slant, only eight investments are recommended:

- Savings accounts
- Term deposits
- Guaranteed Investment Certificates (GICs)
- Canada Savings Bonds (CSBs)
- T-Bills
- Strip bonds
- Fixed-income investment funds
- Equity investment funds

Each of these investment types is designed to achieve a particular investment objective, such as maximizing after-tax return over the long term or providing good liquidity, and they are all readily available. The nature of each investment is relatively easy to understand and none will spring any great surprises on you. All can be selected for ownership inside an RRSP. Interest, and occasionally dividend, income is eligible for your $1,000 investment income deduction as long as the income is Canadian. The eight investments vary as to their rates of return, their risk and their liquidity, or ease with which you can convert each to cash. The first four investments are readily available through financial institutions such as banks, trust companies, credit unions and *caisses populaires*. All can be acquired through a stockbroker. Units in an investment fund often are available from the fund itself.

Savings Accounts

These are available where you bank. Investment dealers and stockbrokers also generally pay daily interest on cash balances. (Some brokers even offer chequing privileges.) The earnings rate, or interest paid on savings or chequing accounts, is generally the lowest of the eight investments and varies with day-to-day changes in prime interest rates. Rates may be slightly better with brokers and at smaller institutions, although your funds could be slightly more at risk. Most banks now offer *investment accounts* that pay a higher rate of interest if a certain amount, perhaps $5,000, is kept on deposit. The interest is eligible for your $1,000 investment income deduction, and it must be included in income for tax purposes, even though you may not receive a T5 slip from the bank.

Savings accounts are the most liquid of the eight investments and are almost risk-free, since they are covered at banks and most trust companies by the $60,000 Canada Deposit Insurance. This protects all your investments (not just savings accounts) at all the branches of one institution to a total of $60,000. It does not apply to each individual investment or each branch of the same institution. Credit unions and *caisses populaires* have their own insurance system which is similar. If an institution fails, you probably will have to wait a considerable period of time before your funds are returned, which may interfere with your plans.

Deposit Receipts (Term Deposits)

These pay interest that is eligible for your $1,000 investment income deduction, are available where you bank, generally in large amounts of $5,000 or more, with terms varying from thirty days to over a year. These are short-term investments designed to be held to maturity, but they can usually be cashed at any time if you are willing to pay a penalty. The degree of liquidity depends on the issuing institution. The earnings rate generally increases as the length of the term to maturity increases. The rates on deposit receipts have, historically, been higher than savings account rates. Rates vary among competing issuers, but the differences are not large.

Deposit receipts are no riskier than savings accounts, so the degree of risk depends on the issuing institution. However, since these are fixed rate investments designed to be held to maturity, there is a minor amount of *term risk* involved. If interest rates increase, the rate of interest on the deposit receipt remains the same, while the interest rate paid on savings accounts and other investments may exceed the rate you are earning on the deposit receipt. This kind of risk would be classified as minimal, however, since these are such short-term investments.

Deposit receipts are included as one of the eight investments only because of their convenience – they are readily available where you bank. However, you can probably get a better return on your short-term funds with T-Bills, Canada Savings Bonds and money market income investment funds. You also should be able to invest smaller amounts.

Guaranteed Investment Certificates (GICs)

These are available where you bank and are also issued by insurance companies. They are interest-bearing investments available in almost any amount with terms ranging from one year to five years and even longer. The interest is eligible for your $1,000 investment income deduction. Unlike deposit receipts, you are generally locked in for the specified term with a GIC. This means that you are not able to cash the security in, even though you may be willing to pay a penalty. However, you can use a GIC as collateral for a loan if necessary. You also might be able to sell the GIC at a discount to a third party. But this general inability to cash a GIC makes them the least liquid of the eight recommended investments.

GICs carry the same degree of risk as savings accounts and deposit receipts, which depends on the issuing institution. However, the term risk of a GIC is considerably greater than any of the other investments because of the locking-in feature. If interest rates increase while you hold a GIC, you could find yourself earning a low rate of interest for a lengthy period of time depending on the maturity date of the GIC. On the other hand, if you expect interest rates to decline, you would generally opt for the longer-term GIC. In this way you could lock in at an interest rate that eventually would be higher than the market rate. Interest rates on longer-term GICs are generally higher than on shorter-term GICs because the term risk is higher.

GICs usually come in two types – one that pays interest periodically, usually semi-annually or annually, and one that accumulates the interest until the maturity date. Two points should be noted about this latter type. First, make sure that the interest earned before the maturity date is reinvested at the stated rate. (With some GICs in RRSPs, the semi-annual interest payment earns income only at savings account rates.) Second, if you have, for example, a five-year GIC, you will have to include the accumulated interest in your taxable income at least every three years – even though you won't actually receive that interest until the maturity date. This requirement, specified under the three-year accrual rules, is discussed in Chapter 5. The amount included in income for tax purposes should be eligible for your $1,000 investment income deduction.

Another point to keep in mind is that if the issuer of a GIC (such as a bank) has not received specific instructions, the amount of cash available on maturity might be deposited to a savings-type account at the institution where it will earn a relatively low rate of interest.

Canada Savings Bonds (CSBs)

Most Canadians have bought, or have considered buying, CSBs at some point, often through a payroll savings plan at their place of employment. CSBs are also available from financial institutions and brokers in denominations of $100 and larger. However, they only go on sale around November 1 of each year, and sales are usually cut off after two or three weeks. An upper annual purchase limit is usually imposed ($75,000 in 1986), although there is no limit to the number of new CSBs you can acquire with cash from old CSBs that mature in that year.

CSBs are interest-bearing investments, the interest being paid annually on November 1, usually by direct deposit to your bank account. There are also compound interest CSBs that pay interest on maturity, usually seven or eight years from the date of purchase. The three-year accrual rules apply to the compound interest bonds. The interest is eligible for your $1,000 investment income deduction.

Keep in mind that the interest rate at which new CSBs are advertised is guaranteed for only one year. After that, the interest on the bond is set each year according to current interest rates, although a minimum rate is guaranteed to be paid to maturity.

CSBs are different from GICs, term deposits and all other bonds, in that they can be cashed in at any time for their face value. You also receive any interest earned up to the end of the preceding month. Thus, if you plan to cash in a CSB, wait until the beginning of a month so you receive the extra interest. If the CSB is cashed before February in the year following the date of purchase (three months), no interest is payable.

Canada Savings Bonds are one of the best short- to medium-term, interest-bearing investments you can make – if you are in the market for such a security during the first two weeks of November. They cannot be purchased at any other time, and there is no secondary market like there is for other bonds. With a CSB, you will participate in any interest rate increases as the government raises the rate payable on the bond periodically to match other rates, but you are protected from significant interest rate declines since a minimum rate is guranteed to be paid on the bond. And if you anticipate that rates will drop, you can cash the CSB and purchase another security, such as a GIC to lock yourself into a high rate for a longer period of time. This combination of an extremely low risk factor, superb flexibility and an attractive interest rate, makes CSBs an almost unbeatable investment in many situations.

T-Bills and Strips

If you deal with a broker, and eventually you should, you will gain ready access to T-Bills and strips, although you might be able to purchase these securities through your banker. T-Bills (Treasury Bills) are short-term interest-bearing securities issued by the federal government. Strips are the semi-annual interest coupons removed from high-quality, long-term government-guaranteed bonds. Both are sold on the discounted face-value principle. In other words, you pay less for the strip or T-Bill than its face value at maturity, and the difference, or discount, is the profit on the strip or T-Bill. This discount is treated as interest for tax purposes and is eligible for your $1,000 investment income deduction.

The size of the discount depends on current interest rates. For example, a strip may promise to pay the owner $6,000 nineteen years from now. If current long-term interest rates are 10%, you will be able to purchase the strip for about $940. This will produce the equivalent of a 10% return compounded semi-annually over the nineteen years you own the strip.

T-Bills work much the same way. If you want to purchase a $5,000 T-Bill that matures in ninety days, and current ninety-day interest rates are 9%, you will pay about $4,890 for the T-Bill and earn interest of $110 over the ninety-day period.

Strips can be acquired in relatively small amounts, but brokers might have a $1,000 to $5,000 minimum for T-Bills. In addition, the broker will charge a small commission for the purchase of strips, and some have begun charging commissions on the purchase of T-Bills.

As can be appreciated, the value of strips and T-Bills will fluctuate depending on interest rates (short-term rates for T-Bills and longer-term rates for strips, which generally are not nearly as volatile as short-term rates). The value of strips or T-Bills that you own increases as the length of time remaining to maturity decreases, but the value will also change depending on current interest rates.

There is an active secondary market for T-Bills, which makes them very *liquid*. This simply means that if you went to sell your T-Bill, even a few days before maturity, you can almost always find a buyer. Your interest is, in effect, credited daily (although it does not compound), since the difference between the purchase and sale price is your interest income from the T-Bill (assuming that interest rates have not changed – see below).

There is a secondary market for strips developing, which means they could also be a relatively liquid investment and you will not necessarily have to hold them until maturity. However, you should consider them to be a long-term investment.

If you sell a strip or T-Bill before maturity, you may realize either a capital gain or a capital loss. Using a $6,000 strip as an example, assume that two years after you buy the strip, long-term interest rates have declined to 8% (leaving seventeen years to maturity). That means that the strip is now worth about $1,580. If interest rates had remained at 10%, the strip would be worth only about $1,140. Thus, if you sell the strip for $1,580, you will be deemed by the tax authorities to have earned interest of $200 ($1,140 minus purchase price of $940) and you will also have realized a capital gain of $440 ($1,580 minus $1,140). The interest is eligible for your $1,000 investment income deduction, while the capital gain is eligible for your $500,000 capital gains exemption.

If interest rates instead climb above 10% after two years and you sell the strip for less than $1,140, your interest income is reduced accordingly. If the strip is sold for less than the purchase price, you will have a capital loss that can only be used to reduce capital gains, which would probably be tax-exempt under the $500,000 capital gains exemption.

Exactly the same principles are applied to the purchase and sale of T-Bills. However, T-Bills are not as risky, because they are short-term investments and therefore interest rate swings will not affect their value as dramatically as strips.

As can be seen from the example, strips can be highly risky investments. A one- or two-percentage point change in interest rates can mean a very large change in the value of your investment.

Since you cannot predict at what interest rate you will be able to reinvest your funds when your strips mature, you should consider buying strips with varying maturities. Strips are subject to the three-year accrual rules and therefore are best held inside an RRSP where they are sheltered from tax.

Investment Funds

Investment funds have become very popular over the past three or four years, particularly as RRSP investments. Financial commentators attribute this new-found appeal to the remarkable performance of the stock market brought about by the economic recovery that began in 1982. As well, more and more people are turning to investment funds in an attempt to simplify their financial affairs. By investing in one or two funds, they participate in a wide variety of investments, something they could not do personally because their resourcs are limited. Thus, they are buying into a balanced portfolio of stocks. More important, perhaps, is the fact that they recognize the value of professional investment advice and are willing to let these experts (the managers of the funds) make investment decisions for them. The financial marketplace has become incredibly complex and sophisticated. One way the average investor can participate alongside the high rollers is through the funds, some of which have done extremely well over the long term.

Very simply, an investment fund is a pool of cash received from investors that is invested by an expert. In theory, this expert will make better decisions than the average investor and therefore achieve a much better earnings rate over the long term. Thus, the average investor is willing to hand over the investing of his or her funds to the expert and will pay the expert an annual fee for the advice.

You purchase units or shares in the fund, at a price that very accurately reflects the market value of the fund's investments at any particular time. In effect, you buy a portion of these investments when you buy units of the fund. In general, then, when the value of the fund's investments goes up, so does the value of the units. The value of these units is reported in the financial pages of larger daily newspapers.

The fund earns investment income throughout the year – interest, dividends and/or capital gains. It also has expenses, including day-to-day operating expenses and fees for the professional management of the investments. Any profit after expenses belongs to the unit holders. With most funds, you have a choice of receiving this profit directly or having it reinvested in units of the fund. In either case, the profit must be included in your income for tax purposes, unless of course the funds are held in your RRSP. Interest, dividends and capital gains retain their identities as they flow through the fund to you.

If you redeem (sell) your units in a fund outside an RRSP, you will realize a capital gain or loss depending on whether you redeem the units for more or less than your purchase price. Any capital gain or loss must be included in income for tax purposes, but gains are eligible for your $500,000 capital gains exemption.

Units in an investment fund can be purchased through your broker and often directly from the fund itself. Most funds require an initial minimum purchase, but subsequent purchases of the particular fund can be made in any amount. Some funds can be purchased on a monthly savings plan and others offer periodic (perhaps monthly) pay-out options that operate like annuities.

All funds charge a fee for the professional management of the investments, ranging from $1/2$% to 2% of the fair market value of the fund annually, and many charge a front-end load fee, which ranges as high as 9% of the purchase price of the units. This fee can usually be reduced by purchasing units of a fund through your broker. The *front-end load* is a fee deducted directly from the purchase price of the units. This fee usually represents the commission paid to the person selling you the fund. The fee also discourages individuals from buying and selling units in a fund over the short term, since the fee is not refundable.

The risk factor of investment funds is more difficult to gauge than the other six investments. Those offered by major financial institutions are at least as secure as the institution itself, as are the larger funds, especially those offered by a major group. Your major concern should be the quality of management and how much confidence you have in the fund's ability to produce the kinds of returns it produced in the past.

There are two basic types of investment funds -- *fixed-income funds* and *equity funds*. Comparatively speaking, equity funds and most income funds are more risky than the other six investments, since you are relying on someone else's decisions to earn a reasonable rate of return and you are not relying on a specific investment to earn a specific rate of return. Equity funds are generally more risky than income funds since the equity fund invests in more risky investments (primarily shares in public corporations). However, over the long term (at least ten years), the risk associated with investment funds declines dramatically, at least if history is any indication, when one examines the average annual returns over the longer period.

Fixed-Income Investment Funds Fixed-income funds invest primarily in a variety of interest-bearing investments. The earnings on your units cannot be predetermined, however, since the value of the fund varies as transactions are made and with movements in interest rates. It is the investments made by the fund that pay a fixed income, such as bonds that pay a specific rate of interest.

Returns depend on the type of income fund you purchase. Income funds can be broken down into three types – *bond funds, money market funds* and *mortgage* or *GIC type funds*. Returns in the better performing bond funds have averaged one or two points above long-term interest rates over the previous ten years, even after deducting management fees. This higher return generally is possible because bond funds realize large capital gains on bonds and other interest-bearing securities when interest rates are declining. However, bond funds do not do as well when interest rates are increasing.

Returns on money market funds, which invest exclusively in short-term securities, are similar to rates on T-Bills and closely follow short-term interest rates over the long term. Returns on the mortgage or GIC type of income fund tend to parallel long-term interest rates. These funds do not have the gains that bond funds realize when interest rates are declining, but they also do somewhat better when interest rates are rising.

The liquidity of an investment in an income fund depends on the particular fund. With most, you can cash your units in the fund fairly quickly, within a few days, although some funds may require a waiting period of up to a month.

Equity Investment Funds Equity funds invest primarily in the shares of public corporations, both Canadian and foreign, and therefore the value of these funds will increase and decrease according to the fair market value of all the fund's assets at the time of valuation. Some equity funds invest primarily in high-quality blue chip shares in order to generate dividends and respectable capital gains. Others invest in more speculative stocks and look for capital gains primarily and dividends only secondarily, while still others invest mostly in preferred shares and earn primarily dividends and little in the way of capital gains.

The liquidity of equity funds is similar to that of income funds. However, all equity funds should definitely be looked at as long-

term investments. Historically, the stock market has outperformed interest-bearing investments by a considerable margin
over the past few decades. You definitely want to hold equity
funds for as long as possible to let history take its course.

The risk factor for equity funds is quite different than that for
most income funds or the other six investments. Equity funds
tend to mirror the performance of the stock market to a greater or
lesser extent (a good equity fund manager will consistently
outperform the stock market by a considerable margin). Thus,
your investment can decline in value if the market declines. On
the other hand, if the stock market is booming, annual gains in
equity funds of 50% are not uncommon. On average, over the
longer term, equity funds handily outperform the other seven
investments. Therefore, the longer you hold an equity fund
investment, the less risk should be involved.

Investment Fund Caution You are cautioned to be aware that all
funds do not perform equally. What is this year's winner may be
next year's loser. You must pick your fund carefully, and in fact
you should hedge your bets by investing in more than one fund.
Some investors will move from fund to fund in order to follow a
manager with a good track record. It is probably safe enough to
invest in two fixed-income funds and three equity funds with a
minimum of $2,000 to $3,000 in each, but do not hesitate to
spread your investment funds around even more.

12
The Financial Security
Formula – Overview

√ = PROBABLY HAVE MOST IMPORTANCE AT THIS TIME
FOR AVERAGE FAMILIES

	A	B	C	D	E
SAFETY NET					
Income replacement (life) insurance – on both spouses if necessary	√	√	√	√	√
Other insurance – disability, mortgage, fire, property, car, etc.		√	√	√	√
Contingency/retirement fund – both spouses			√	√	√
Wills, power of attorney – review periodically	√	√	√	√	√
HOME					
Savings program for purchase of first home	√				
Pay down the mortgage		√	√	√	√
Purchase a vacation property(?)				√	√
Borrow against equity only to fund children's education if necessary				√	

	A	B	C	D	E
RETIREMENT SAVINGS					
Maximize RRSP contributions – both spouses	✓	✓	✓	✓	✓
Use RRSP only for purchase of first home	✓				
Maximize $1,000 investment income deduction – both spouses			✓	✓	✓
Maximize $500,000 capital gains exemption – both spouses				✓	✓
Balance investment portfolio – in favour of equities	✓	✓	✓	✓	
– in favour of interest-bearing securities					✓
Review benefits of company-sponsored pension plans		✓	✓	✓	✓
CHILDREN'S EDUCATION					
Invest family allowance payments in children's names			✓	✓	
Invest children's own income				✓	
Children 15 or older — deferred interest GICs				✓	

A = Pre-home, pre-children
B = First home, no children
C = Home and young children
D = Home and older children
E = Empty nest

Appendix A
A Sample Scorecard

A model for a yearly scorecard is presented below. It is a simple net worth statement that is relatively conservative in nature. It does not include the value of your furniture and appliances, jewellery, paintings, antiques, stamp collections, etc. in your net worth total, since these can easily give you a false sense of security. Most people overvalue their possessions, sometimes by outlandish amounts, and few people will part with most of their treasures, except in the most dire of emergencies. And in any case, most amateurs are poor investors in these types of items.

The numbers in the scorecard (shown in Table A.1) are representative of a couple in their mid-forties with two children close to college age. The eldest will enter university next year. They have regularly made RRSP contributions and have paid down some of the mortgage on their home. They have also made a particular effort to save for their children's university education since both could be in school at the same time for at least one year. The husband and wife are working full-time, and both children work part-time to help with their education, so the couple manages to devote $16,400 of their combined incomes to achieving the four basic financial objectives.

The scorecard is easy to use. You simply add in the amounts from your work-related income devoted to the four goals, add the income earned on investments in the year or the increase in value (deduct losses or decreases in value), and deduct amounts that have been used for other purposes which reduce your wealth. The balance at the end of the year is the opening balance at the beginning of the next year.

Table A-1

	Value (Equity in) at Beginning of Year	Contributions to, Additions, Debt Reduction, Mortgage Pay Down	Income (Loss) During the Year After Taxes, Increase (Decrease) in Value	Wealth Reduction, Savings Used for Various Purposes	Value (Equity In) at End of Year
RETIREMENT (Step 3)					
–RRSP					
–Company Plan (Only if Measurable)	$98,000	$10,800	$18,500		$127,300
–Other					
HOME (Steps 2 and 4)					
–Principal	70,000	2,000	12,000		84,000
–Vacation					
RETIREMENT/CONTINGENCY (Step 5)					
–$1,000 Investment Income Deduction	7,000	1,000	700	$5,000 (car purchase)	3,700
–Other					
ADDITIONAL RETIREMENT (Step 6)					
–$500,000 Capital Gains Exemption	9,000	1,000	2,200		12,200
–Other					
CHILDREN'S EDUCATION (Step 7)					
–Family Allowance	14,000	600	1,600		16,200
–Children's Earnings	6,000	1,000	600		7,600
–Other					
TOTAL	$204,000	16,400	35,600	($5,000)	$251,000

For example, the couple had $7,000 in their retirement contingency fund at the beginning of the year (funds earning interest income eligible for the $1,000 investment income deduction) and added another $1,000 to the fund at the beginning of the year. Tax-free interest of $700 was earned, but towards the end of the year, they removed $5,000 from the fund to help with the purchase of a new car. Thus, $3,700 was left in the contingency fund ($7,000 plus $1,000 plus $700 minus $5,000 = $3,700). Over the next few years, much larger amounts will be removed from accumulated wealth to finance their children's education.

Note that the average after-tax return during the year, ignoring tax that eventually will be payable with the RRSP, was about 16% on the opening balance of $204,000 plus additions of $16,400. Their increase in wealth during the year was about 23% on the opening balance.

Appendix B

What the 1985/86 Pension Reforms Will Mean to You

The pension reform proposals introduced in 1985 and 1986 are scheduled for implementation in 1987 and 1988. They have been a decade in the making. It appears that all pension plans will be affected, since the provinces have agreed in principle to institute reforms almost identical to the federal pension reforms. Still unresolved, however, is the nagging question of indexing pension benefits to increases in the cost of living.

The reform proposals should make pensions more accessible to more Canadians, enabling them to provide adequately for their retirement years without undue dependence on the government. In fact, if you and your spouse make maximum pension contributions to your company plan and/or personal RRSPs starting at age thirty, you should have no problem retiring comfortably by the time you are sixty or sixty-five, with an indexed retirement income more or less comparable to your average family income just before retiring. This assumes that your home is paid off, you collect the maximum benefits from the Canada Pension Plan, and that all pension contributions are made to take full advantage of the new, more generous limits.

Pension Reform Proposals

The pension reform proposals focus on three primary areas: putting all pension plans on the same footing, making pension plans more accessible to more workers and improving benefits for a large number of workers. There are three major types of pension plans: employer-sponsored defined benefit plans, employer-sponsored money purchase plans, and self-contributory Registered Retirement Savings Plans (RRSPs) – also considered to be money purchase plans, which were originally designed to act as a pension plan for the self-employed and for employees who do not have access to a company-sponsored plan. Deferred Profit-Sharing Plans (DPSPs) also benefit from pension reform.

Under a defined benefit RPP (Registered Pension Plan), a certain pension is guaranteed to be paid. The employer, with or without the financial help of the employee, provides the necessary funding to pay the required pension. Under money purchase plans, the employee and the employer contribute to the plan, and the best pension possible is purchased with the accumulated funds in the plan when the employee retires.

Non-Contributory Reforms

The major non-contributory, or pension standards, reforms affecting employer-sponsored RPPs take effect January 1, 1987, and include:

Eligibility for Membership Full-time workers will be eligible to join a plan after two years of service with the employer, and part-time workers will be able to join after they have earned at least 35% of the average industrial wage in each of two consecutive years.

Vesting (the time at which the employee attains the right to pension benefits resulting from both his or her and the employer's contributions). Vesting will occur after the employee has been a member of the plan for two years no matter what the employee's age, instead of the standard ten years or age forty-five.

Refunding On termination of employment, the employee's contributions that have not vested must be returned, plus a reasonable rate of interest.

Employer's Contributions The employer must pay for at least half the value of any pension earned under a defined benefit plan, which generally means the employer must, at a minimum, contribute as much to the plan as the employee. Alternatively, in some jurisdictions the employer has the option of providing indexed benefits under the plan.

Portability When changing employers, employees will generally be able to choose from several options: (a) leave their vested pension benefits on account with their former employer and eventually receive a pension; (b) receive an early pension if they are within ten years of the normal retirement date specified in the pension plan; (c) transfer their pension entitlement to their new employer; or (d) transfer their benefits to a locked-in RRSP – a variation on normal RRSPs, where the employee will not have access to the RRSP funds except to receive a retirement income.

Early Retirement Pension plans will allow for early retirement ten years prior to the normal retirement age stated in the plan.

Survivor Benefits A plan must provide for benefits to continue to be paid to a surviving spouse at a minimum of 60% of the full benefit rate, even if the spouse remarries; a surviving spouse is also entitled to the full accrued benefits of a plan member who dies before retirement.

Women's Pensions Every pension plan must guarantee to pay the same benefits to men and women retiring under the same circumstances.

Marriage Breakdown All plans must permit the splitting of pension benefit entitlements between spouses on the breakdown of their marriage.

Information Disclosure Plans must provide information about earned benefits and accumulated contributions to members and their spouses every year. As well, a majority of plan members may require representation by members and pensioners on pension management committees.

Inflation Protection Although inflation protection has not been legislated, Ontario is rumoured to be considering it in its provincial pension standards legislation.

Contributory Reforms

The intent of the pension reform is to put RRSPs and other money purchase Registered Pension Plans (RPPs) on the same footing as defined benefit RPPs, at least as far as contributing and providing pension benefits. In the past, defined benefit RPPs have provided much larger maximum pension benefits than money purchase plans, which include RRSPs and DPSPs. The employee's maximum annual pension from a defined benefit RPP is determined as the lesser of the following (to a maximum of $60,025):

- $1,715 times the number of years of pensionable service not exceeding thirty-five years, or
- 2% for each year of pensionable service (to a maximum thirty-five years), times the average of the best three consecutive years of remuneration.

This pension can be indexed to increases in the cost of living, but no more than $60,025 can be paid in the first year of retirement that the pension is received.

Under money purchase RPPs, the contribution limits before 1987 for both the employee and employer were $3,500, for a maximum of $7,000 annually; almost invariably this would produce a smaller maximum pension than that available with a defined benefit plan.

Contributions allowed to an RRSP were even smaller. Before 1986, they were limited each year to 20% of earned income, to a maximum of $5,500 ($7,500 in 1986 and 1987). If the employee were eligible for benefits from a company pension plan, he or she was limited to contributing 20% of earned income to a maximum of only $3,500, less all contributions the employee made to the RPP.

Using current, reasonable actuarial assumptions, the government has determined that a contribution of $15,500 a year for thirty-five years would result in a pension of about $60,000 a year. It then decided to put RRSPs and other money purchase plans on the same footing as defined benefit plans by improving the contribution limits.

Additional Technical Details of RRSPs

As discussed in Chapter 6, RRSP contributions beginning in 1988 are limited to 18% of earned income in the previous year up to a specific dollar maximum (referred to as RRSP *contribution room*), less contributions made to, or benefits accrued in the year under other pension plans (this amount is called the *pension adjustment*, or *PA*). The dollar maximums are phased in as follows:

1988 – $ 9,500
1989 – $11,500
1990 – $13,500
1991 – $15,500

Indexing of the $15,500 figure will be reconsidered in light of tax reform expected to be introduced over the next two or three years. Beginning in 1989, you will be able to carry forward unused contribution room to the following seven years. Therefore, in any particular year, you will be able to contribute an amount consisting of your current year's contribution limit plus any contribution room existing from any of the previous seven years after 1987 (total contribution room).

Persons who are not members of an RPP or DPSP will have no PA and will be able to contribute the maximum allowed. Persons who belong to money purchase RPPs or DPSPs must reduce their RRSP contribution room by the amount they and their employer have contributed to the RPP or DPSP in the previous year.

Persons who belong to defined benefit RPPs are in a different position. Their RRSP contribution room is reduced by an amount that reflects the value of contribution room taken up by the RPP in the previous year. The PA in this case is calculated generally as: (9 times Benefit Entitlement) minus $600.

The *nine times factor* recognizes that, on average, it takes approximately nine dollars to fund every one dollar of pension income annually on retirement. The $600 is an *ad hoc* figure that has been established in recognition of the fact that not all pension plans provide the same benefits. The benefit entitlement represents the pension benefit accrued during the previous year. It is based on the structure of the particular plan. For example, if a plan has a single benefit rate of 1.5% of the best average three consecutive years, and the employee's pensionable earnings over the whole year (generally salary or wages) are $38,000, the benefit entitlement will be calculated as follows:

Benefit entitlement = .015 (1.5%) × $38,000 = $570

The PA would then be calculated as:

PA = (9 × $570) – $600 = $4,530.

The employee's RRSP contribution room in 1988 would be the lesser of $9,500 and 18% of $38,000 minus PA of $4,530 equals $2,310.

If the employee were entitled to a maximum pension of 2% of pensionable earnings, his or her maximum allowable RRSP contribution would be only $600. Not all defined benefit RPPs are the same, so adjustments to the PA calculation will be made.

The new system is extremely complicated for defined benefit RPP members, but fortunately, employers will be required to report an employee's PA to Revenue Canada each year and Revenue Canada will then advise the employee, and every taxpayer for that matter, of his or her total RRSP contribution room, including eligible room for the years after 1988 to a maximum of seven previous years. You will be notified of eligible contribution sometime late in the year, which will give you enough time to make an RRSP contribution before the March 1 deadline of the following year. Actually this deadline only applies to contribution room that is about to expire because more than seven years will have passed. This will not be a concern until March 1, 1996.

One problem with the new system is that employees who are members of pension plans will have to estimate their contribution room if they want to make a contribution before being advised by Revenue Canada of the exact figure. As explained in Chapter 6, you should try to make your RRSP contributions as early in the year as possible. Once the system is operational and you know your PA from the previous year and how it was calculated, you might be able to estimate reasonably accurately your PA for the current year, since you will know your previous year's earnings upon which the PA is based. Employees should try to encourage their employers to provide a PA as early in the year as possible. This should be easy to do if the benefits under the RPP do not change from year to year.

Two other adjustments can be made to total contribution room available in any given year. Benefits in respect of prior years after 1986 (past service credits) under your company-sponsored pension plan can only be increased to the extent of total RRSP contribution room available. If past service RPP benefits are increased, RRSP contribution room is adjusted downward correspondingly (called the past service pension adjustment – PSPA).

Occasionally, RPP benefits may be reduced or eliminated; for example, you may leave your job and receive a refund of RPP contributions because your benefits have not vested. In this situation, total RRSP contribution room can be restored under the pension adjustment reversal (PAR) mechanism.

Transfers of Pension Income to RRSPs

Beginning in 1990, you will no longer be allowed to transfer on a tax-free basis the following "pension" amounts to your RRSP:

- Canada/Quebec Pension Plan payments
- Old Age Security payments
- Pension benefits paid periodically from an employer-sponsored RPP
- Periodic payments from a Deferred Profit-Sharing Plan (DPSP)
- Retirement income from an RRSP (also cannot be transferred to an RPP or a Registered Retirement Income Fund (RRIF).

However, from 1990 to 1994 inclusive, you will be able to transfer up to $6,000 of payments from an RPP to an RRSP of which your spouse is the annuitant. In addition, beginning in 1987, the tax-free transfer of retiring allowance payments to an RRSP is restricted to a maximum of $2,000 for each year of service after 1986.

Changes to Registered Pension Plans

The following are the major changes affecting RPP contributions made by members of company-sponsored plans:

- The deductible contribution limit to defined benefit RPPs was removed beginning in 1986; however, since employers must fund at least half the benefits available under a plan, employees should generally be contributing less than half of $15,500 (the dollar amount estimated to be necessary to fund maximum pension benefits under a defined benefit plan).
- The combined employer and employee deductible

contribution limit for money purchase RPPs is increased in stages as follows:

1987 – $ 9,500
1988 – $11,500
1989 – $13,500
1990 – $15,500

- Additional voluntary contributions (AVCs) to money purchase plans were eliminated in 1986. Employees now must use RRSPs to gain any extra pension benefits, and only within the prescribed limits.
- The seven-year carry-forward rules are available to all taxpayers through an RRSP. The equivalent to a seven-year carry forward may be available under a defined benefit RPP (past service credits) to the extent of RRSP contribution room available, but is restricted by the terms of the particular plan. RRSP contribution room is reduced accordingly.

Employee Responsibility

Most members of company-sponsored RPPs and all people who contribute to RRSPs will be affected, at least to some degree, by pension reform. Almost all workers will be better off. However, with better benefits and more flexibility comes more responsibility placed on you, the worker. There will be a much greater onus on you to understand your pension plan and its benefits, and to maximize new and additional benefits when changes are made to the plan over the next five years, and in particular when you change jobs. You should make a point to become as familiar with the new rules as possible and see what benefits you can ultimately derive. By early 1987, once legislation has been released to implement many of the reform measures, a great deal of reliable information should be available both from the government and the private sector. If you and your fellow employees feel you are not being served well by your current plan, now may be the time for you to approach your employer and suggest an overhaul since the company will be reviewing its pension plan in any case to ensure it conforms with the new pension rules.

As money purchase RPPs become more popular, and as you begin contributing larger and larger amounts to your RRSP, you will have to shoulder more responsibility for the earnings in these plans. A spread of just 2% in average earnings over the long term could result in your pension either being doubled or cut in half. You and your fellow employees should take an active interest in your pension plan. Find out what the current earnings are and compare this with the earnings of other plans and RRSPs. If you are unhappy, discuss with your employer the possibility of moving the pension funds to a new trustee or administrator with a better performance record. Or perhaps you may be better off choosing to contribute to an RRSP as long as your employer's pension plan contributions are converted into salary.

Deferred Profit-Sharing Plans

The contribution rules for DPSPs will come into effect in 1988 under the pension reform. The maximum contribution that will be allowed is the lesser of 18% of the employee's wages and $7,750. This limit will be phased in as follows:

> 1988 $5,750
> 1989 $6,750
> 1990 $7,750

No employee contributions are allowed and the maximum RRSP contributions allowed must be reduced by any DPSP contributions made by the employer. In other words, your PA includes employer DPSP contributions.

Certain other features of DPSPs will be tightened up under pension reform so that the employee's vested benefits under a plan are not at as great a risk as they can be now in some circumstances. Most notably, restrictions will be placed on the purchase of shares by the DPSP in the employer corporation.

Appendix C
Calculating Potential Returns on Investments

The four tables on the following pages will help you determine the expected return on your investments over various lengths of time.

Annual Savings Program 1 (Table C.1) This table calculates the amount accumulated at the end of a particular year if $1 is saved at the beginning of each year and the earnings compounded annually. For example, suppose you decide to save family allowance payments of $400 at the beginning of each year for eighteen years. You expect a return after-tax of 11% compounded annually. You will accumulate $22,375.60, determined by multiplying $400 times 55.939, which is taken from Table C.1 at the intersection of 11% and 18 years.

If you put your money into a less risky investment such as Canada Savings Bonds that earn 8% after taxes each year, you would accumulate $16,178.40 ($400 times 40.446). If you accept more risk and invest in an equity fund that earns 20% a year compounded annually, you will accumulate $61,496.00 ($400 times 153.740). Now you can ask yourself if this much larger amount accumulated is worth the increased risk.

If the earnings on your investment are taxable each year, you first must subtract the tax paid before calculating the total accumulation. For example, you expect to earn 12% by investing the family allowance payments, but tax is payable on the earnings at the rate of 25% each year. Therefore, your after-tax earnings rate is actually 9% annually (12% minus tax [25% of 12% equals 3%] which is 12% minus 3% equals 9%). Thus, $18,007.20 will be accumulated at the end of eighteen years ($400 times 45.018).

Table C.1: Future Value – Annual Investing

Calculates the amount accumulated at the end of a particular year if the earnings compound annually and $1 is saved at the beginning of each year.

	8%	9%	10%	11%	12%	15%	20%
1	1.080	1.090	1.100	1.110	1.120	1.150	1.200
2	2.246	2.278	2.310	2.342	2.374	2.472	2.640
3	3.506	3.573	3.641	3.710	3.779	3.993	4.368
4	4.867	4.985	5.105	5.228	5.353	5.742	6.442
5	6.336	6.523	6.716	6.913	7.115	7.754	8.930
6	7.923	8.200	8.487	8.783	9.089	10.067	11.916
7	9.637	10.028	10.436	10.859	11.300	12.727	15.499
8	11.488	12.021	12.579	13.164	13.776	15.786	19.799
9	13.487	14.193	14.937	15.722	16.549	19.304	24.959
10	15.645	16.560	17.531	18.561	19.655	23.349	31.150
11	17.977	19.141	20.384	21.713	23.133	28.002	38.581
12	20.495	21.953	23.523	25.212	27.029	33.352	47.497
13	23.215	25.019	26.975	29.095	31.393	39.505	58.196
14	26.152	28.361	30.772	33.405	36.280	46.580	71.035
15	29.324	32.003	34.950	38.190	41.753	54.717	86.442
16	32.750	35.974	39.545	43.501	47.884	64.075	104.931
17	36.450	40.301	44.599	49.396	54.750	74.836	127.117
18	40.446	45.018	50.159	55.939	62.440	87.212	153.740
19	44.762	50.160	56.275	63.203	71.052	101.444	185.688
20	49.423	55.765	63.002	71.265	80.699	117.810	224.026
25	78.954	92.324	108.182	126.999	149.334	244.712	566.377
30	122.346	148.575	180.943	220.913	270.293	499.957	1,418.258
35	186.102	235.125	298.127	379.164	483.463	1,013.346	3,538.009
40	279.781	368.292	486.852	645.827	859.142	2,045.954	8,812.629

Annual Savings Program II (Table C.2) This table calculates the amount you must save at the beginning of each year to accumulate $1,000 at the end of a particular period if the earnings compounded annually. For example, suppose that you want to take a year off work to go back to school after your children leave home. This will not occur for twenty-five years, but you expect that you will need about $80,000 (in future year's dollars) at that point to finance the year off. You expect to earn 15% annually after-tax. To accumulate $80,000 at the end of twenty-five years, you must save $326.88 at the beginning of each year. This calcula-

Table C.2: Specific Value – Annual Investing

Calculates the amount you must save at the beginning of each year to accumulate $1,000 at the end of a particular period if the earnings compound annually.

	8%	9%	10%	11%	12%	15%	20%
1	925.926	917.431	909.091	900.901	892.857	869.565	833.333
2	445.157	438.962	432.900	426.967	421.159	404.449	378.788
3	285.216	279.867	274.650	269.561	264.597	250.415	228.938
4	205.482	200.613	195.883	191.285	186.816	174.144	155.241
5	157.830	153.296	148.907	144.658	140.544	128.970	111.983
6	126.218	121.945	117.825	113.853	110.023	99.336	83.921
7	103.771	99.716	95.823	92.086	88.498	78.574	64.520
8	87.051	83.188	79.495	75.965	72.592	63.348	50.508
9	74.148	70.458	66.946	63.605	60.428	51.804	40.066
10	63.916	60.385	57.041	53.875	50.879	42.828	32.102
11	55.626	52.245	49.057	46.055	43.228	35.712	25.920
12	48.792	45.551	42.512	39.664	36.997	29.983	21.059
13	43.076	39.969	37.071	34.370	31.855	25.313	17.183
14	38.238	35.260	32.497	29.935	27.564	21.468	14.078
15	34.101	31.247	28.613	26.185	23.950	18.276	11.568
16	30.534	27.798	25.288	22.988	20.884	15.607	9.530
17	27.435	24.813	22.422	20.245	18.265	13.362	7.867
18	24.724	22.213	19.937	17.876	16.015	11.466	6.504
19	22.340	19.936	17.770	15.822	14.074	9.858	5.385
20	20.234	17.933	15.872	14.032	12.392	8.488	4.464
25	12.666	10.831	9.244	7.874	6.696	4.086	1.766
30	8.174	6.731	5.527	4.527	3.700	2.000	.705
35	5.373	4.253	3.354	2.637	2.068	0.987	.283
40	3.574	2.715	2.054	1.548	1.164	0.489	.114

tion is performed by multiplying 4.086 (taken from Table C.2 at the intersection of 15% and 25 years) times 80 (the number by which $1,000 must be multiplied to get $80,000). You can determine what $80,000 is in today's dollars by using Table C-4.

Table C.2 can also be used for determining how much you have to save each year for the down payment on your first home. You have determined that you will need $25,000 in six years and you expect to earn 9% after-tax. Therefore, you must save $3,048.63 at the beginning of each year to accumulate the $25,000 (25 times 121.945).

The numbers in Table C.2 can also be used to demonstrate how easy it is to build up large amounts in your RRSP if you start saving early in your working career. For example, suppose that you are thirty years old and you want $2 million in your RRSP by the time you are seventy (in other words, forty years from now). You will invest in an equity fund that earns 15% compounded annually. You must save only $978 at the beginning of each year to become a millionaire twice over (2,000 times 0.489).

Lump-Sum Savings I (Table C.3) This table allows you to calculate how much accumulates by the end of a particular year if earnings compound annually and a $1 lump sum is saved at the beginning of Year 1. For example, suppose that you have inherited $8,000 from Aunt Matilda and you want to put it towards your children's post-secondary education. The $8,000 will earn 12% after-tax and will be used at the end of fourteen years. You will accumulate $39,096 ($8,000 times 4.887 – the number intersecting 14 years and 12% in Table C.3).

You could also use the table to determine how much you might accumulate if you put an extra $500 aside for your retirement when you are twenty-five years old. You put the $500 in an equity fund where it will earn 20% compounded annually after-tax. At the end of forty years when you are sixty-five, you will have $734,886 ($500 times 1,469.772).

Table C.3: Future Value – Lump Sum

Calculates how much accumulates by the end of a particular year if the earnings compound annually and a $1 lump-sum is saved at the beginning of year one.

	4%	6%	8%	10%	12%	15%	20%
1	1.040	1.060	1.080	1.100	1.120	1.150	1.200
2	1.082	1.124	1.166	1.210	1.254	1.323	1.440
3	1.125	1.191	1.260	1.331	1.405	1.521	1.728
4	1.170	1.262	1.360	1.464	1.574	1.749	2.074
5	1.217	1.338	1.469	1.611	1.762	2.011	2.488
6	1.265	1.419	1.587	1.772	1.974	2.313	2.986
7	1.316	1.504	1.714	1.949	2.211	2.660	3.583
8	1.369	1.594	1.851	2.144	2.476	3.059	4.300
9	1.423	1.689	1.999	2.358	2.773	3.518	5.160
10	1.480	1.791	2.159	2.594	3.106	4.046	6.192
11	1.539	1.898	2.332	2.853	3.479	4.652	7.430
12	1.601	2.012	2.518	3.138	3.896	5.350	8.916
13	1.665	2.133	2.720	3.452	4.363	6.153	10.699
14	1.732	2.261	2.937	3.797	4.887	7.076	12.839
15	1.801	2.397	3.172	4.177	5.474	8.137	15.407
16	1.873	2.540	3.426	4.595	6.130	9.358	18.488
17	1.948	2.693	3.700	5.054	6.866	10.761	22.186
18	2.026	2.854	3.996	5.560	7.690	12.375	26.623
19	2.107	3.026	4.316	6.116	8.613	14.232	31.948
20	2.191	3.207	4.661	6.727	9.646	16.367	38.338
25	2.666	4.292	6.848	10.835	17.000	32.919	95.396
30	3.243	5.743	10.063	17.449	29.960	66.212	237.376
35	3.946	7.686	14.785	28.102	52.800	133.176	590.668
40	4.801	10.286	21.725	45.259	93.051	267.864	1,469.772

Lump-Sum Savings II and Inflation – Table C.4 This table calculates the lump-sum amount that you must save at the beginning of Year 1 to accumulate $1 at the end of the particular period if earnings compound annually. For example, you think that you might like to retire a year early for some extended travel, but you want to

205

Table C.4: Specific Value – Lump Sum

Calculates the lump-sum amount that you must save at the beginning of year one to accumulate $1 at the end of the particular period if earnings compound annually.

	4%	6%	8%	10%	12%	15%	20%
1	.96154	.94340	.92593	.90909	.89286	.86957	.83333
2	.92456	.89000	.85734	.82645	.79719	.75614	.69444
3	.88900	.83962	.79383	.75131	.71178	.65752	.57870
4	.85480	.79209	.73503	.68301	.63552	.57175	.48225
5	.82193	.74726	.68058	.62092	.56743	.49718	.40188
6	.79031	.70496	.63017	.56447	.50663	.43233	.33490
7	.75992	.66506	.58349	.51316	.45235	.37594	.27908
8	.73069	.62741	.54027	.46651	.40388	.32690	.23257
9	.70259	.59190	.50025	.42410	.36061	.28426	.19381
10	.67556	.55839	.46319	.38554	.32197	.24718	.16151
11	.64958	.52679	.42888	.35049	.28748	.21494	.13459
12	.62460	.49697	.39711	.31863	.25668	.18691	.11216
13	.60057	.46884	.36770	.28966	.22917	.16253	.09346
14	.57748	.44230	.34046	.26333	.20462	.14133	.07789
15	.55526	.41727	.31524	.23939	.18270	.12289	.06491
16	.53391	.39365	.29189	.21763	.16312	.10686	.05409
17	.51337	.37136	.27027	.19784	.14564	.09293	.04507
18	.49363	.35034	.25025	.17986	.13004	.08081	.03756
19	.47464	.33051	.23171	.16351	.11611	.07027	.03130
20	.45639	.31180	.21455	.14864	.10367	.06110	.02608
25	.37512	.23300	.14602	.09230	.05882	.03034	.01048
30	.30832	.17411	.09938	.05731	.03338	.01510	.00421
35	.25342	.13011	.06763	.03558	.01894	.00751	.00169
40	.20829	.09722	.04603	.02209	.01075	.00373	.00068

postpone collecting your pension until your normal retirement date. To accumulate $90,000 in thirteen years, how much must you save now if you can earn 15% after-tax? Using the number shown in Table C.4 where 13 years and 15% intersect, $90,000 is multiplied by 0.16253, which means that you must put away $14,627.70 now to save the $90,000.

The table will also calculate what $90,000 is in today's dollars. If you think inflation will average 4% over the thirteen-year period, $90,000 is worth $54,051.30 in today's dollars ($90,000 times 0.60057). If you think inflation will average 6%, it is worth only $42,195.60 ($90,000 times 0.46884). Thus, the higher you think the inflation rate will be, the less the future dollars will be worth in today's dollars.

Going back to one of the previous examples where the twenty-year-old put away $500 that earned 20% over forty years and grew to $734,886, how much is this worth in today's dollars? The following inflation rates are assumed:

4% inflation $734,886 × 0.20829 = $153,069.40
6% inflation $734,886 × 0.09722 = $71,445.60
8% inflation $734,886 × 0.04603 = $33,826.80

You should note that a doubling of the inflation rate to 8% from 4% cuts the value expressed in today's dollars by 80%. In other words, if the inflation rate doubles, you will be only one-fifth as well off. The magic of compounding operates on inflation too, except in reverse.

Glossary

Accrued income Income earned and credited to you, but not considered to be received for tax purposes. Also called *deferred income*. Interest may accrue on GICs or capital gains may accrue on equity fund investments.

Allowable capital loss For tax purposes, calculated as 50% of a capital loss.

Amortization Generally, the period of time over which a debt is allocated or spread out. Mortgages may be amortized over twenty-five years, which means if you stick to the repayment schedule you will pay off your mortgage in exactly twenty-five years.

Annuitant The person who receives payments from an annuity; also the person who will eventually receive retirement income from an RRSP.

Annuity A financial instrument, usually purchased with a large sum, that provides periodic payment of principal and interest over a particular length of time.

Arm's length Describes a transaction where there is no special relationship among interested parties that would cause them to ignore fair market value.

Assessment notice Official notification of your tax liability from Revenue Canada.

Attribution rules Tax legislation that, in certain instances, makes you taxable on income earned on assets which you have transferred to your spouse or to a child under eighteen years of age.

Bear market A general decline in the value of publicly traded shares on the stock market.

Beneficiary Person entitled to the funds from an insurance policy when the insured person dies; also the person entitled to benefit from a trust or other financial arrangement.

Blue chip stocks The shares of large, well-established corporations with a history of good earnings and dividend payments.

Bull market A general increase in the value of publicly traded shares on the stock market.

Canada Deposit Insurance Insurance carried by banks and most trust companies protecting individual depositors against losses up to a total of $60,000.

Capital gain or loss The difference between the sale price of a capital property and the purchase price after allowing for all costs of purchase and sale.

Capital property Securities or physical property, such as real estate, that may increase or decrease in value and on which a gain or loss may be realized on disposition.

Cash surrender value The value of a permanent, or whole life, insurance policy if it is cancelled. Term policies have no value except on the death of the insured.

Collateral Property pledged as security for a loan. A mortgage is simply a loan with your home as collateral. If you default on the loan, the mortgagee (the bank) can sell your home to recover the amount of the loan.

Consumer Price Index (CPI) Measures month-to-month changes in the cost of living or inflation.

Common shares Shares that represent a portion of ownership in a corporation allowing owners of those shares to participate in the increase or decrease in the fortunes of the company. May have voting rights and dividends may be paid on the shares.

Deferred income Income already earned but not yet reported for tax purposes.

Dividend tax credit Reduces the amount of personal tax paid on dividends from Canadian corporations; intended to compensate for tax already paid by the corporation paying the dividend.

Employee benefit Non-monetary compensation from employer. Many employee benefits are taxable, in which case they are given a monetary value and are considered to be part of the employee's wage subject to tax.

Equity Ownership interest in a property. Can be represented by shares in a corporation, the value of which reflect the changing worth of the company.

Face amount Amount stated on a life insurance policy to be paid if the insured should die.

Fair market value The amount that a willing buyer would pay and a willing seller would accept in an open and unrestricted market, assuming that both parties are knowledgeable, are dealing at arm's length, and neither is under any compulsion to act.

Fixed income Rate of return stated on an investment to be earned over a particular period of time; not applicable to income investment funds that may invest in fixed-income investments.

Front-end load A sales charge, or commission, applied on the purchase of units in an investment fund; deducted from the amount invested.

Gross-up of dividends Method of calculation which reduces taxes payable on Canadian dividend income.

Group life insurance Policy issued to an employer for the benefit of employees. Its face value is often limited to $25,000, in which case the employee is not considered to have received a taxable benefit.

Indexing Periodic increases in a series of payments, often tied to a specific percentage or to increases in the Consumer Price Index.

Joint and last survivor annuity An annuity under which payments continue to either person named as an annuitant, even after the death of one of the persons named.

Leverage Using borrowed money to increase the amount invested and, hopefully, the rate of return on an investment.

Liquidity A measure of how readily an investment can be converted to cash, without incurring either a penalty or a loss in the value of the investment.

Margin Situation where you borrow from your broker for the purchase of securities which are, in effect, lodged as collateral against the loan. The term *margin* refers to the amount of cash put up by the investor for the purchase.

Marginal rate of tax Tax rate applied to the last dollar of income earned in the year, which is the portion of income that is taxed most heavily.

Money market Part of the capital market devoted to short-term lending and borrowing of money.

Mutual funds Simply another name for *investment funds.*

Net income For tax purposes, the amount determined after deducting RRSP and pension plan contributions, tuition fees and various other expenses, but before deducting personal exemptions, the $1,000 investment income deduction and the $500,000 capital gains exemption.

Opportunity cost Also called *alternative investment cost.* The amount you could have earned if you had chosen to invest your funds elsewhere.

Personal exemptions Amounts deducted from net income on your tax return for yourself and dependants.

Portfolio All the securities owned by an individual, whether inside or outside an RRSP. A home is considered part of a portfolio for purposes of the financial security formula because, for many Canadians, it is their most significant investment.

Preferred shares Issued by a corporation after the distribution of common shares. Preferred shares carry dividends at specific rates, which must be paid before dividends are paid on common shares.

Present value The value of something in the future expressed in terms of its value today. Present value is used in financial circles to ensure that dollars in the future are measured and therefore compared accurately. A dollar in 1990 and 1998 will not have the same purchasing power. If both are expressed in terms of their value in 1987, they can be compared meaningfully.

Prime lending rate The lowest interest rate at which banks lend money, usually to their best customers. The rate at which you can borrow may be expressed as prime plus a specific percent. Only the best credit risks (usually large corporations) can borrow at prime.

Principal residence The tax term for the home that you own and in which you live. Any gain realized on the sale of your home is tax-exempt. Families are allowed this exemption on only one owner-occupied home after 1981, but for gains arising before 1982, each spouse may claim an exemption on one owner-occupied home, which could include a vacation property.

Prospectus A legal document describing securities being offered for sale to the public. Investment funds must generally be sold *by prospectus*, which simply means you must be furnished with a copy of the prospectus of the particular fund before you can buy units in the fund for the first time.

Registered Retirement Income Fund (RRIF) A vehicle for generating retirement income. Must be purchased with RRSP funds, and in fact operates much like an RRSP, except a minimum amount must be paid out each year.

Stock options Generally, an agreement under which you agree to purchase shares at some future date at a price agreed upon now. The option itself may have a value and, indeed, some options are actively traded.

Tax instalments Tax payments that must be made every three months to Revenue Canada by individuals who are self-employed or have a substantial amount of investment income.

Taxable capital gain One-half a capital gain. Exempt from tax under the lifetime $500,000 capital gains exemption.

Taxable income The total amount of your income, less all eligible deductions. Tax is calculated on this figure.

Trust Very simply, the holding of property (usually investments) by one person (the trustee) for the benefit of another person (the beneficiary). A *settlor* transfers the property to the trustee (often the same person). A properly established trust is considered a separate entity for tax purposes.

Index